STATUS REPORT

on the

ENVIRONMENTAL JUSTICE COLLABORATIVE MODEL: A FRAMEWORK TO ENSURE LOCAL PROBLEM-SOLVING

**Developed by
Federal Interagency Working Group
On Environmental Justice**

Office of Environmental Justice
Office of Enforcement and Compliance Assurance
U.S. Environmental Protection Agency
Washington, DC 20460

Preface

In May, 2000, the 11 federal agencies comprising the Federal Interagency Working Group on Environmental Justice (IWG) developed and issued an Interagency Environmental Justice Action Agenda (Action Agenda). The goals of the Action Agenda are as follows:

(1) to promote greater coordination and cooperation among federal agencies;

(2) to make government more accessible and responsive to communities;

(3) to initiate environmental justice demonstration projects to develop integrated place-based models for addressing community quality-of-life issues; and

(4) to ensure integration of environmental justice in policies, programs and activities of federal agencies.

The underlying premise of the Action Agenda is that a collaborative model is an effective method for comprehensively and proactively addressing the interrelated environmental, public health, economic, and social concerns collectively known as environmental justice issues. The IWG, in partnership with various stakeholders (i.e., state, tribal, and local government agencies; community organizations; industry representatives; and others) established 15 demonstration projects to test this underlying premise.

This interim status report presents a "work-in-progress" as it:

(1) summarizes the "lessons learned" from the ongoing projects;

(2) identifies the elements of success;

(3) examines the emerging outline of a coherent collaborative problem-solving model; and

(4) describes efforts to evaluate the model and specific demonstration projects.

These activities are intended to lay the groundwork for a second round of IWG demonstration projects being identified for 2002.

The collaborative efforts described in this report have as a theme the federal government's responsibility for assuring that all Americans live in high quality environments. This theme follows a key principle of the National Environmental Policy Act (NEPA) of 1969, in which Congress wrote that it is the continuing responsibility of the federal government to assure that all Americans live in "safe, healthful and aesthetically and culturally pleasing surroundings." This Congressional mandate is also clearly reflected and referenced in EPA Administrator Christine Todd Whitman's August 9, 2001 memorandum regarding the Agency's continuing commitment to environmental justice. Administrator Whitman stated that: "Environmental justice is achieved when everyone, regardless of race, culture, or income, enjoys the same degree of protection from environmental and health hazards **and** equal access to the decision-making process to have a healthy environment in which to live, learn, and work." As Chair of the IWG, Administrator Whitman stated that the Office of Environmental Justice is dedicated to ensuring that mandate is fulfilled within the Agency and supporting the efforts of other federal agencies that comprise the IWG to pursue the same mandate.

Most importantly, the IWG demonstration projects and the collaborative model have received enthusiastic and widespread endorsement from all stakeholder groups. For example, according to the National Environmental Policy Commission's *Report to the Congressional Black Caucus and Congressional Black Caucus Foundation Environmental Justice Braintrust* (September 28, 2001, Washington, DC), "The IWG demonstration projects are particularly significant. They point to the potential to problem-solve across stakeholder groups in a constructive, collaborative manner, building relationships, avoiding duplicated efforts, and leveraging instead of wasting resources." The IWG's work last year on the demonstration projects has forged an important new integrated prototype for federal agencies and stakeholders in the area of creative, collaborative, and constructive problem-solving.

Table of Contents

Table of Figures

Summary: The Federal Interagency Working Group on Environmental Justice (IWG) is supporting and evaluating 15 demonstration projects to investigate and demonstrate whether collaborative, integrated problem-solving can succeed in building partnerships and local capacity to resolve local environmental justice problems. Each project is unique because conditions and capacities varied widely. This Status Report provides information on the implementation of these projects and outlines the characteristics common to successful models with the goal of promoting widespread replication.

Introduction: This report summarizes the lessons learned from the implementation of the Interagency Environmental Justice Action Agenda (Action Agenda)[1] during the past year. The Federal Interagency Working Group on Environmental Justice (IWG),[2] designed the Action Agenda to create dynamic and proactive partnerships among community-based organizations, business and industry, non-governmental organizations, and government at all levels to help communities address local environmental justice issues.

Fifteen demonstration projects comprise the core of the Action Agenda. Lessons learned from these demonstration projects will be used by concerned stakeholders to help promote and support the development of collaborative integrated problem-solving mechanisms. The IWG projects designed these mechanisms to comprehensively address the range of interrelated environmental, public health, economic, and social concerns that collectively are known as environmental justice issues.[3] When EPA announced the Action Agenda on May 24, 2000, stakeholders in the

---

[1] The "Integrated Federal Interagency Environmental Justice Action Agenda" was developed by the Interagency Working Group on Environmental Justice and published by EPA, EPA document #300-R-00-008, November 2000.
[2] The Interagency Working Group on Environmental Justice was mandated by Executive Order 12898, "Federal Actions to Address Environmental Justice in Minority Populations and Low-Income Populations," issued February 11, 1994, 59 Fed. Reg. 7629. The IWG is chaired by the U.S. Environmental Protection Agency.
[3] EPA defines environmental justice as "the fair treatment and meaningful involvement of all people regardless of race, color, national origin, culture, education, or income with respect to the development, implementation and enforcement of environmental laws, regulations and policies. *Fair treatment* means that no group of people, including racial, ethnic or socioeconomic group should bear a disproportionate share of the negative environmental consequences resulting from industrial, municipal and commercial operations or the execution of federal, state, local or tribal programs and policies. *Meaningful involvement* means that: (1) potentially affected community residents have an appropriate opportunity to participate in decisions about a proposed activity that will affect their environment and/or health; (2) the public's contribution can influence the regulatory agency's decisions; (3) the concerns of all participants involved will be considered in the decision-making process; and (4) the decision-makers seek out and facilitate the involvement of those potentially affected." *EPA Guide to Assessing and Addressing Allegations of Environmental Injustice*, (Working Draft, January 16, 2001).

environmental justice dialogue had a limited understanding of a systematic and holistic model for engaging in collaborative problem-solving.[4] As a result of implementing the Action Agenda,

Figure 1. Implementation of Environmental Justice at federal agencies

a coherent model is beginning to emerge. Therefore, a primary purpose of this report is to document the elements of this emerging collaborative model so that partners can share the approach and promote its widespread replication.

The Action Agenda demonstration projects follow the strategy of collaborative and constructive problem-solving advocated by the EPA Office of Environmental Justice (OEJ). Each

---

[4] While no systematic understanding of a collaborative model existed, the concept was not new. For example, the National Advisory Council on Environmental Policy and Technology developed the Integrative Environmental Justice Model Demonstration Approach in 1993. Additionally, the City of Clearwater, Florida, in 1996, began developing a model environmental justice strategic plan for brownfields redevelopment.

demonstration project involves coordination among two or more federal agencies acting in partnership with an array of local stakeholders, such as: community-based organizations; industry; civic and faith-based groups; academic institutions; state, local, and tribal governments; and philanthropic organizations. The goal of these demonstration projects is improved quality-of-life for residents in communities of concern by enhancing the capacity of local parties to work together for shared goals. The IWG intends the demonstration projects to: (1) promote federal support of solutions that begin in the community and remain in the community; (2) link federal, state, local, and tribal local government with comprehensive community-based planning processes; (3) coordinate activities of multiple government and private entities to use resources more efficiently; (4) develop a template for integrated and holistic local solutions to environmental justice issues; and (5) serve as a platform for advocating and demonstrating innovation in government at all levels.

The demonstration projects and their associated partnerships are voluntary. The diverse underlying interests of the many parties involved (e.g., resolution of longstanding disputes, serving as a good corporate citizen, and improving environmental quality) create a sufficient basis and motivation for collaborative problem-solving. From a federal perspective, these demonstration projects encourage better leveraging of existing federal resources through improved coordination among agencies, and increased community and other stakeholder participation.

To date, these 15 demonstration projects have accomplished a wide range of successes, including the following:

- Establishing strong working partnerships of more than 150 organizations and 11 federal agencies;
- Securing commitments of more than $15 million in public and private funding to address issues ranging from children's health to economic revitalization;
- Augmenting existing brownfields redevelopment initiatives to fully meet quality-of-life and economic development needs in diverse communities;
- Using innovative approaches to foster local capacity- and partnership-building through

reliance upon community and faith-based organizations, development of community-based planning and vision, and leveraging of existing resources;

- Using alternative dispute resolution and consensus building to address, as appropriate, cases of conflict or potential conflict;

- Addressing children's health concerns in six minority, low-income and tribal communities; and

- Identifying some key elements of a systematic model for holistic, integrated, and collaborative problem-solving.

Environmental Justice Demonstration Projects

Figure 2. Locations of Demonstration Projects

Background: Executive Order 12898 created the IWG. The Executive Order delineates the IWG agency responsibilities as follows: "To the extent practicable and permitted by law, and consistent with the principles set forth in the report on the National Performance Review, each federal agency shall make achieving environmental justice part of its mission by identifying and addressing, as appropriate, disproportionately high and adverse human health or environmental effects of its programs, policies, and activities on minority populations and low-income populations...."Additionally, the Executive Order calls for the IWG to "develop interagency model projects on environmental justice that evidence cooperation among agencies." On May 24, 2000, EPA announced that a group of diverse organizations, confronting protracted environmental justice problems, committed themselves to working toward solutions through participation in one of 15 national environmental justice demonstration projects.

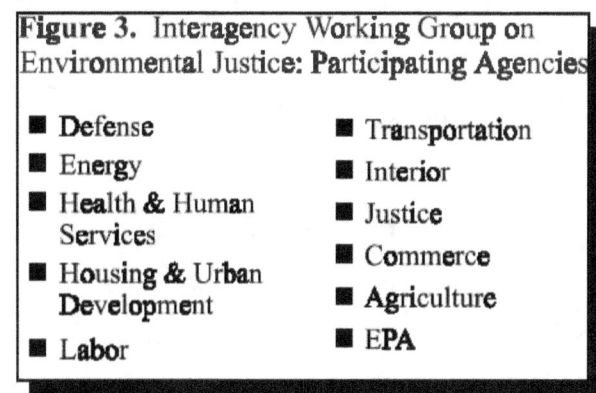

Figure 3. Interagency Working Group on Environmental Justice: Participating Agencies

- Defense
- Energy
- Health & Human Services
- Housing & Urban Development
- Labor
- Transportation
- Interior
- Justice
- Commerce
- Agriculture
- EPA

Defining the Need: The demonstration projects were needed by communities with environmental justice issues to provide models of collaborative integrated problem-solving that can result in long-term improvements in the quality-of-life. The IWG sponsored the demonstration projects to establish processes that can better target, utilize, and leverage existing resources. Better interagency coordination is critical to improving the capacity for addressing, at the local level, the range of interrelated environmental, public health, economic, and social concerns that typically constitute environmental justice issues. Too often, environmental justice issues reach the federal government in the form of seemingly intractable, multifaceted, and multi-layered disputes. By the time environmental justice issues become recognized as such by the federal government, they tend to: (1) cut across agency jurisdictions or areas of expertise; (2) involve many stakeholders holding mutually inconsistent perspectives about the nature of the issues confronting them; and (3) involve parties having longstanding, adversarial relationships.

While parties may occasionally resolve their disputes in a win-win manner, through collaborative and cooperative processes, they do not sufficiently document these "success stories" or sufficiently disseminate them for others to benefit from their experience. Traditionally, courts or administrative tribunals decide the cases which become visible, and one side seems to prevail at the other's expense. While recognizing that all communities and situations are different, and that collaborative processes are not always appropriate, stakeholders do not typically explore proactive, collaborative pathways to resolution.

Towards a Solution: The IWG has focused on three activities to foster the emergence of a coherent collaborative problem-solving model: (1) nurture and promote local demonstration projects; (2) promote a national dialogue on collaborative models; and (3) identify the elements of success for developing a coherent collaborative model.

- **Nurture and promote local demonstration projects:** The IWG demonstration projects foster proactive, collaborative efforts that bring agencies, at all levels of government, together with diverse stakeholders in impacted communities. Together at the same table for the first time, in some cases, participants: (1) better understand each other's perspectives; (2) identify mutual interests and priorities; and (3) with this boarder and shared view, mobilize existing resources (i.e., social, human, and financial) for the purpose of creating win-win solutions.

- **Promote national dialogue on building collaborative models:** The IWG is promoting a national dialogue on building collaborative models to achieve environmental justice goals. This dialogue is intended to foster a consensus among all stakeholder groups around the appropriate use of a

Figure 4. International City/County Management Association (ICMA) Forum on Building Collaborative Models to Achieve Environmental Justice

collaborative model. Another goal is to inform all stakeholder groups, particularly those confronting environmental justice issues, about opportunities to utilize a collaborative model. IWG members have conducted meetings and briefings for community, business, industry, faith-based groups, and state, local, and tribal government partners, and other stakeholders. This sharing of information and lessons learned has helped to identify potential new partnerships and build interest in applying a collaborative model.[5]

- **Identify elements of success for developing a coherent collaborative model:** The IWG, through the efforts of the EPA Office of Policy, Economics, and Innovation, is undertaking an evaluation for the IWG collaborative model. This evaluation is intended to: (1) identify and study critical elements that contribute to the success of the collaborative problem-solving model in each project; and (2) analyze the effectiveness of the collaborative problem-solving model and its constituent elements to optimize performance in the future.

These activities have been instrumental in creating a common understanding of collaborative models to achieve environmental justice across the gamut of stakeholders. It is important to create a deeper understanding of the mechanisms involved and to help diverse stakeholders in impacted communities to understand the value and benefits of this voluntary and cooperative approach. Without a common understanding of the appropriate use and value of these models, stakeholders will lack the knowledge they need to overcome historical mistrust and adversarial relationships.

An Emerging Collaborative Model: The purpose of this section of the report is twofold: (1) to identify the basic elements common to all the collaborative models which are emerging from the demonstration projects; and (2) to describe the evaluation of the collaborative model. The IWG

---

[5] The American Indian and Alaska Native Environmental Justice Roundtable (Albuquerque, New Mexico, August 3-4, 2000) assembled a representative group of American Indians, Alaska Natives, environmental protection experts, legal scholars, ethicists, tribal elders, religious leaders, cultural specialists, policy experts, and others from around the country to identify and address the issues associated with environmental justice in Indian Country.

intends that this two-pronged strategy produce a template that a community-based organization, academic institution, business or industry, or government, or any other group can utilize as a collaborative problem-solving model.

Elements of Success of Collaborative Model:[6] The basic elements common to all the collaborative models can be grouped into five categories:

- Issue Identification and Leadership Formation;
- Capacity- and Partnership-Building;
- Strategic Planning and Vision;
- Implementation; and
- Identification and Replication of Best Practices.

The model is dynamic, cyclical, and iterative. Because it is dynamic, several elements may take place concurrently and recurrently. In addition, new ideas will emerge and new parties will join in as efforts gain momentum.

Issue Identification and Leadership Formation: Long-standing concerns in the impacted community tend to surface from the efforts of one individual or a small group of individuals who are particularly active in the community. These concerns can include "substantive issues" such as high asthma rates, children suffering lead poisoning, undesirable land uses, proximity of residences to noxious facilities, lack of

> *Three individual rural townships in agricultural New Madrid County, Missouri approached federal agencies about lead exposure, drinking water quality, and pesticide hazards that pose risks to children's health. Upon hearing of each other's concerns, the townships determined that their concerns were related and they developed a partnership to leverage resources and benefits of their individual and collective knowledge. This process of learning that they confronted similar problems led to the establishment of the New Madrid County Tri-Community Child Health Champion Project. [Issue Identification and Leadership Formation]*

---

[6] The elements identified for the environmental justice collaborative model are based upon the experience to date of the demonstration projects as well as the literature in the field of community development and community building. These range from Singer, Molly, *Righting the Wrong: A Model Plan for Environmental Justice in Brownfields Redevelopment* (Washington, DC: International City/County Management Association, 2001) to the *Community Collaborative Wellness Tool* (Washington, DC: Together We Can, 1998). The latter tool provides for five stages, i.e., 1. Getting Together, 2. Building Trust and Ownership, 3. Strategic Planning, 4. Taking Action, and 5. Deepening and Broadening the Work.

parks and recreational areas, and lack of employment opportunities. These concerns also can include "process issues" such as the need to strengthen public participation, leadership, improved education of stakeholders, and trust among stakeholder groups to work together. Depending on the ability of diverse stakeholders in a community to respond collectively ("social capital"[7]), and the importance, clarity, and complexity of the concerns articulated, community organizations and other stakeholders may need assistance to arrive at a common understanding of these concerns. When these concerns have matured into a salient issue, or a set of issues, the parties typically elicit the support of a set of initial partners, make an assessment of whether or not conditions are ripe for collaboration, and crystallize an initial vision of the nature of the issue and how to address it.

> *While Latinos in the United States are disproportionately impacted by asthma, the rates of asthma of Latinos of Puerto Rican descent are greater than Latinos of Cuban or Mexican descent. In an effort to better understand this phenomenon, the EPA, U.S. Health Resources Service Administration (HRSA), Robert Woods Johnson Foundation, and Mt. Sinai Medical Center convened an action-oriented conference in New York. This was followed by a meeting in Puerto Rico that was cosponsored by EPA, HRSA, the Puerto Rico Department of Health, and the Asthma Coalition of Puerto Rico. These two meetings were attended by over 1000 people and led to the formation of a comprehensive strategy by the Asthma Coalition of Puerto Rico to combat this serious illness. [Issue Identification and Leadership Formation]*

Elements to Foster Issue Identification and Leadership Formation:
- Build upon existing leadership and expertise in the impacted communities;
- Conduct local education and outreach efforts, fact-finding and assessments;
- Involve residents early in identifying concerns and crystallizing issue;
- Identify early on potential partners from all stakeholder groups;

---

[7] The term "social capital" was used by Jane Jacobs in her book, *The Death and Life of Great American Cities* (New York: Random House, 1961) and was popularized by Harvard sociologist Robert D. Putnam in his book, *Making Democracy Work: Civic Traditions in Modern Italy* (Princeton: Princeton University Press, 1993). Putnam defines social capital as the "features of social organization such as networks, norms, and social trust that facilitate coordination and cooperation for mutual benefit." The World Bank refers to social capital as "not just the sum of the institutions which underpin a society—it is the glue that holds them together."

- Build upon a strong understanding of community history and practices; and
- Assess whether or not conditions are ripe for collaboration.

Capacity- and Partnership-Building:

Capacity- and partnership-building allow stakeholders to work cooperatively on issues of mutual concern and to identify and more effectively mobilize the resources needed. Capacity-building needs differ, depending on stakeholders and issues. Capacity is the ability of an individual or organization to undertake an effort and achieve it effectively. For example, while community groups may need support to work effectively with government agencies, industry-based stakeholders may require training or assistance to work effectively with communities. Well-structured partnerships assemble the needed capacity to resolve issues. Partnerships involving multiple stakeholder groups, with different strengths and abilities, enable the participants to match the right tool or ability to the appropriate task.

> *A facilitator assisted 20 diverse organizations—both public and private—in Barrio Logan, a low-income Latino community in San Diego, California to design a formal partnership agreement. Barrio Logan has been plagued by substandard housing, incompatible land uses, air pollution, overcrowded schools, lack of adequate health care and social services, and high unemployment rates. As an organized partnership, the organizations are poised to access and collectively utilize the resources and skills of all the partners. The partners have decided to support designation of the community as a pilot "Urban Village", an initiative which would bring a major infusion of City of San Diego planning and infrastructure resources to the community. In addition, the U.S. Department of Housing and Urban Development is working with the City of San Diego to apply for a one million dollar grant on lead hazard controls for Barrio Logan. [Capacity- and Partnership-Building]*

Elements to Foster Capacity- and Partnership-Building:
- Build upon existing organizational capacity in the impacted communities;
- Establish dialogue leading to possible partnerships with all relevant stakeholders/parties, including community, business, and government;
- Secure commitments from multiple, appropriate federal, state, local, and tribal agencies and seek to ensure adequate government coordination, internally, as well

as with non-government parties;

- Foster capacity through training, mentoring, technical assistance, or resource support;
- Provide consensus-oriented facilitation services, where necessary;
- Design processes, both formal and informal, to help ensure fair treatment and meaningful participation of all stakeholders;
- Develop processes that help ensure community education and capacity building in the future; and
- Establish processes that allow for inclusion of new partners as they emerge.

Strategic Planning and Vision:

A fundamental premise of the collaborative model is to link government, at all levels, with comprehensive, community-based planning processes. The IWG defines "community-based planning" as a process that enables a community to identify its assets, aspirations, needs, and limitations with sufficient clarity to then apply and leverage its resources (e.g., technical,

Re-Genesis, a community-based organization, worked with its 1400 members to create a comprehensive vision for cleaning up and revitalizing their communities of Arkwright and Forest Park in Spartanburg, South Carolina. Re-Genesis mobilized all parties to address the environmental and health issues, initially through cleanup efforts and more recently through revitalization plans. Benefits envisioned include housing, technology and job-training centers, a greenway, and a health clinic. The local government, Chamber of Commerce, and federal elected officials are working with Harold Mitchell, President of Re-Genesis, to turn this vision into reality. Recently, Re-Genesis and a local chemical facility entered into a formal facilitation process to resolve their differing visions for future land use in the area. [Strategic Planning and Vision]

organizational, and financial) consistent with one plan to make meaningful and quantifiable progress toward achieving the plan's stated goals.

Elements to Foster Strategic Planning and Vision:

- Facilitate articulation of, and build upon, community vision of its aspirations;
- Determine community assets (e.g., technical, financial, social, cultural, natural resources) and deficits (e.g., environmental conditions, infrastructure,

unemployment);

- Utilize different tools for incorporating comprehensive community planning into project (e.g., Geographic Information Systems, planning charettes);

- Identify, target and leverage assets from all sources (e.g., community, government, industry, academia); and

- Reinforce community values while building human and social capital and entering implementation phase.

Executive Director Mary Nelson's motto for Bethel New Life, a faith-based community development corporation, is "turning environmental liabilities into community assets and opportunities." Having identified contaminated properties in the abandoned industrial neighborhood of West Garfield in Chicago, Illinois, she is leading the effort to bring innovative, energy efficient, environmentally friendly technology to the development of a major mixed-use development. The project will be located at a major transit stop that will provide the surrounding community with convenient access to the local rail line. This effort will provide the community with a child development center, medical clinic, bank, drug store, and other commercial spaces. [Strategic Planning and Vision]

Implementation: Realizing a vision to address identified issues requires well-defined objectives, timelines and action plans. All partners must articulate and follow through commitments, even voluntary commitments, for the project to: (1) address the identified issues thoroughly; (2) strengthen and maintain partnerships; and (3) realize the shared goals.

Elements to Foster Implementation:

- Develop strategies tailored to communities' assets and

The Metlakatla Indian Community Master Plan envisions the cleanup, restoration, and reuse of the Metlakatla Peninsula in southeastern Alaska. To implement this master plan, Tribal Environmental Coordinator Jeff Benson's task was to investigate the extent of environmental pollution. Starting out with his pickup truck as the tribe's environmental office, Benson and environmental engineer Callie Ridolfi identified and mapped 87 contaminated sites requiring cleanup at several formerly used defense facilities and a government operated airfield. They found extensive soil contamination around some of the fuel storage sites, the existence of open dumps, and contamination at building sites at these facilities. Their efforts resulted in federal designation of the Metlakatla Indian Community as a National Brownfields Showcase Community. [Implementation]

deficits;

- Design projects to meet the strength of partnerships, resources and the capacity of the partners;

- Produce clearly defined, well thought-out action plans;

- Identify, nurture, and promote collaborations with win/win scenarios;

- Identify and build upon small successes;

- Ensure clear commitments on the part of all partners.

- Ensure resolution of conflicts or potential conflicts through use of alternative dispute resolution;

- Cluster and order tasks to promote efficient use of time and resources;

- Develop methodology to measure and evaluate the impact on community and stakeholder conditions as projects are undertaken;

- Add to and strengthen partnerships as new issues and relationships are understood; and

- Build community and organizational capacity through implementation to facilitate next phase.

> *Community-based organizations in heavily congested New York City neighborhoods are suffering from poor air quality resulting in high rates of respiratory illnesses. These organizations are working with city, state and federal agencies to have government vehicles converted to use of cleaner fuels in their neighborhoods. This has resulted in a commitment by the US Postal Service of $1.93 million to purchase 55 electric and natural gas vehicles. The project partners have successfully leveraged the benefits of pollution reduction by placing the clean fuel vehicles where they are needed most. [Implementation]*

Identification and Replication of Best Practices: Key to deepening and sustaining the work is the ability to sum up progress in quantitative, qualitative, institutional, and social terms and to incorporate lessons learned into a continuous process. Lessons learned need to be shared not only with the project community, but also with other communities and stakeholders so that best practices can be replicated broadly.

> *As a result of the knowledge gained from the initial East St. Louis demonstration project, the scope of the project has expanded beyond lead testing and abatement to developing a partnership with area Brownfields efforts. East St. Louis was selected to be a National Brownfields Showcase Community. The natural synergies between the environmental justice and brownfields issues has led to a multi-pronged strategy around improved health, economic development and overall quality of life. [Identification and Replication of Best Practices]*

Elements to Foster Identification and Replication of Best Practices:

- Clearly define measures of success of project objectives, process, outputs, institutional effects, and quality-of-life results;
- Understand and evaluate, from different stakeholder perspectives, indicators used to measure success;
- Develop a "template" for successful collaborative models, based on experience in specific community;
- Develop mechanisms to integrate the lessons into future efforts as new issues and challenges are identified; and
- Share, publish, and disseminate experiences and lessons learned.

Evaluation of Environmental Justice Collaborative Model: The EPA Office of Policy, Economics and Innovation (OPEI) is conducting an evaluation of the IWG environmental justice collaborative model. The evaluation will be based upon case studies of selected demonstration projects. The evaluation will:

(1) identify and study critical elements that contribute to the success of the collaborative problem-solving model in each project; and

(2) analyze the effectiveness of the collaborative problem-solving model and its constituent elements to optimize performance in the future.

This evaluation will provide information to create more effective and efficient applications of a collaborative model in the future. As illustrated below, OPEI will analyze each project using the following project "logic," in terms of: (1) objectives; (2) process; (3) outputs; (4) institutional effects; and (5) environmental and other outcomes.[8]

Objectives → Process → Outputs → Institutional Effects → Environmental Outcomes*

↑ ↑

External Factors

* "Environmental outcomes" include environmental, public health, social, and quality of life outcomes.

Figure 5. Collaborative Model Evaluation Process

The following tables provide examples of how the above project logic will be applied.

	Objectives	Process	Outputs	Institutional Effects	Environmental and Other Outcomes
Measures	Build capacity of residents to address EJ issues by conducting lead screening and abatement in distressed community.	Federal partners will work with local government, health care and educational institutions, and neighborhood organizations to achieve objectives.	Identify areas of high risk for lead exposure in East St. Louis, conduct community education, abate lead in soil, and identify opportunities for beneficial reuse of land.	Greater cooperation will emerge between all stakeholders.	Youth protected from environmental contaminants.
Key Questions	Are the project objectives clear to all participants?	Was a process in place to allow for effective coordination?	Did the project perform its stated objectives?	Did greater cooperation emerge among all stakeholders?	What percentage of youth was protected from lead as a result of the project?

Figure 6. Identifying Measures and Key Questions Using a Project Logic for the East St. Louis Demonstration Project

---

[8] By "environmental outcomes", we are referring to "environment" in the broader sense, including environmental, public health, social, and quality of life outcomes.

To arrive at truly win-win scenarios for all stakeholders, evaluation will have to take into account the greatly varied perspectives held by the stakeholders involved in any project.

Through analysis at each phase, the projects will be evaluated to determine how the stakeholders' goals are being met. This can be illustrated as follows:

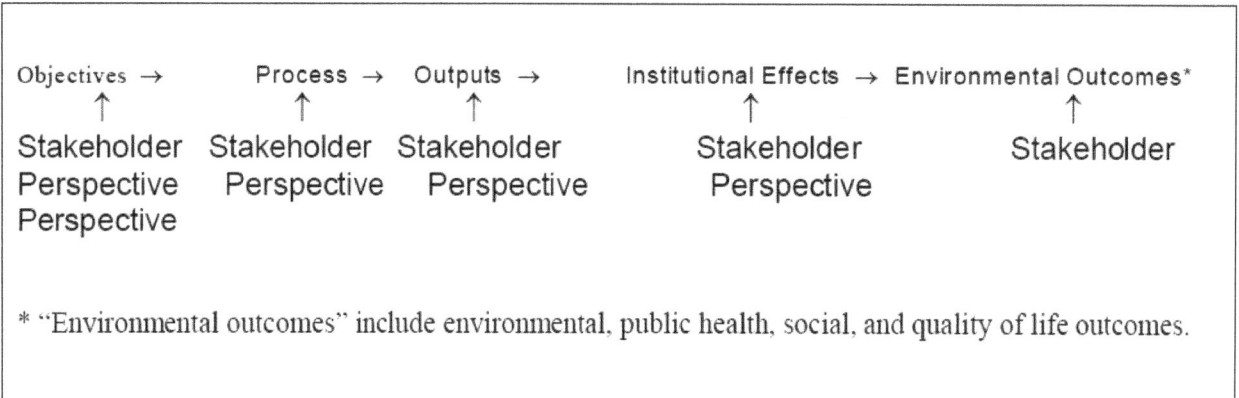

Objectives →   Process →   Outputs →   Institutional Effects → Environmental Outcomes*

Stakeholder   Stakeholder   Stakeholder   Stakeholder   Stakeholder
Perspective   Perspective   Perspective   Perspective
Perspective

* "Environmental outcomes" include environmental, public health, social, and quality of life outcomes.

Figure 7. Understanding Stakeholder Perspectives

	Objectives	Process	Outputs	Institutional Effects	Environmental and Other Outcomes
Measures	Build capacity of residents to address EJ issues by conducting lead screening and abatement in distressed community.	Federal partners will work with local government, health care and educational institutions, and neighborhood organizations to achieve objectives.	Identify areas of high risk for lead exposure in East St. Louis, conduct community education, abate lead in soil, and identify opportunities for beneficial reuse of land.	Greater cooperation will emerge between all stakeholders.	Youth protected from environmental contaminants.
Key Questions	How satisfied are stakeholders with the project objectives? Are these the right objectives?	How satisfied are participants with the coordination between stakeholders?	How satisfied are stakeholders with the project activity? Are these the right activities?	What was the effect of multi-stakeholder collaboration?	Are the outcomes sufficient to address the underlying issues?

Figure 8. Understanding Stakeholder Perspectives in the East St. Louis EJ Project

OPEI will produce a report based upon case studies of selected projects by early 2002. Lessons learned will be used to better design, implement, evaluate, and promote future collaborative problem-solving efforts.

Conclusion: The desire and commitment of the more than 150 parties and 11 federal agencies to participate in the national environmental justice demonstration projects underscores the potential to create a problem-solving methodology capable of addressing environmental justice issues. While we are cognizant that not all environmental justice issues are good candidates for collaborative processes, progress to date has shown that in a short period of time the demonstration projects have achieved measurably improved conditions through locally organized cooperative efforts. Although the circumstances of each project and the issues to be addressed are different, the shared elements used to achieve progress in meeting goals suggests that an underlying, replicable model for integrated, collaborative problem-solving can be identified.

Indeed, the set of environmental, economic, public health and social concerns known as environmental justice issues are perhaps some of the most complex challenges to the nation. More than two decades of experience has shown that no one group can achieve its goals alone because in most cases the success of one stakeholder group is dependent on the success of others. It, therefore, gives all stakeholders in the environmental justice dialogue great hope that the vision of a collaborative problem-solving process has progressed to the point where successful partnerships are mapping their contours. This will go a long way toward making the potential for collaborative and constructive problem-solving a reality for all communities.

FEDERAL INTERAGENCY WORKGROUP ON ENVIRONMENTAL JUSTICE
KEY CONTACTS

AGENCY	NAME	TELEPHONE	E-MAIL
US EPA/OEJ	Charles Lee Associate Director, OEJ Policy, Interagency Liaison Environmental Protection Agency	202/564-2597 Fax: 202/501-1163	lee.charles@epa.gov
DOC/NOAA	Roan Conrad Director Office of Sustainable Development and Intergovernmental Affairs, National Oceanic and Atmospheric Administration Department of Commerce	202/482-3384 Fax: 202/482-2663	roan.conrad@noaa.gov
DOD	Len Richeson Environmental Protection Specialist, Office of the Deputy Under Secretary of Defense Department of Defense	703/604-0518 Fax:703/607-4237	len.richeson@osd.mil
DOE	Melinda Downing Environmental Justice Program Manager Office of Environmental Management Department of Energy	202/586-7703 Fax: 202/586-0293	melinda.downing@em.doe.gov
DOJ	Quentin C. Pair Attorney Environmental Enforcement Section Department of Justice	202/514-1999 Fax: 202/514-0097	quentin.pair@usdoj.gov
DOI	Willie R. Taylor Director Office of Environmental Policy and Compliance Department of Interior	202/208-3891 Fax: 202/208-6970	willie_taylor@ios.doi.gov
DOI/BIA	Clifford Mahooty Environmental Engineer and Environmental Justice Coordinator Bureau of Indian Affairs, Department of Interior	505/346-7223 Fax: 505/346-2543	cliffmahooty@bia.gov

FEDERAL INTERAGENCY WORKGROUP ON ENVIRONMENTAL JUSTICE
KEY CONTACTS

AGENCY	NAME	TELEPHONE	E-MAIL
DOL	Babette D. Williams Environmental Justice Coordinator Office of the Assistant Secretary Department of Labor	202/693-5910 Fax: 202/693-5960	williams-babette@dol.gov
DOT	Marc Brenman Senior Policy Advisor for Civil Rights Federal Highway Administration Department of Transportation	202/366-1119 Fax: 202/366-9371	marc.brenman@ost.dot.gov
HHS/ATSDR	Rueben Warren Associate Administrator for Urban Affairs, ATSDR Health and Human Services	404/498-0111 Fax: 404/498-0087	rcw4@cdc.gov
HHS/NIEHS	Charles Wells Director Environmental Justice, Health Disparity and Public Health National Institute of Environmental Health Sciences Health and Human Services	301/496-2920 Fax: 301/496-0563	wells1@niehs.nih.gov
HUD	Antoinette G. Sebastian Senior Community Environmental Planner, Office of Environment and Energy Housing and Urban Development	202/708-0614 x4458 Fax: 202/ 708-3363	antoinette_sebastian@hud.gov
OMB	Carol Dennis Senior Attorney Environment Branch Office of Management and Budget	202/395-4822 Fax: 202/395-5836	cdennis@omb.eop.gov
USDA/US Forest Service	Robert Ragos Title VI & Related Program Manager, USFS US Department of Agriculture	202/205-0961 Fax: 202/690-2510	rragos@fs.fed.us
CNS	David Miller Environment Sector Specialist Corporation for National and Community Service Agency	202/606-5000 x.491 Fax: 202/208-4151	dmiller@cns.gov

Appendix II

INDIVIDUAL INTERAGENCY DEMONSTRATION PROJECT REPORTS

Table of Contents

Appendix II

INDIVIDUAL INTERAGENCY DEMONSTRATION PROJECT REPORTS

INDIVIDUAL INTERAGENCY DEMONSTRATION PROJECT REPORTS

Re-Genesis: Cleanup and Revitalization through Collaborative Partnerships, Arkwright and Forest Park Community

Spartanburg, South Carolina   *Lead Agency: Environmental Protection Agency*

The project has enabled Re-Genesis, a community-based organization in the Arkwright/Forest Park area of Spartanburg, South Carolina, to establish a broad and dynamic public-private partnership to foster identification, inventory, assessment, cleanup and redevelopment of contaminated sites. The project committee, which is chaired by Re-Genesis, the City of Spartanburg and the County of Spartanburg, consists of many federal agencies, business and industry, non-governmental organizations, academic institutions, South Carolina Department of Health and Environmental Control, and elected officials. It is engaged in a process of stakeholder education, structured dialogues, and planning charettes to create short- and long-term development strategies.

The City of Spartanburg, South Carolina has a population of 43,687. Approximately 53 percent of the population is white and 46 percent is African American. The target area —Arkwright/Forest Park on the south side of the city—has a 96 percent African American population. The target community is within a one-quarter-mile radius of two Superfund sites. Other local areas of concern include an abandoned textile mill, an operating chemical plant, two dumps, and several suspected illegal disposal areas. These properties have brought concerns about public safety, blight, health, and the environment for some time. The area has not enjoyed any substantial commercial development for years, and the vast majority of normal retail needs are not within close proximity.

Re-Genesis, an active, community-based group with 1,400 members, has taken the lead in establishing partnerships to address local environmental and health issues as well as revitalization. Numerous community meetings and forums have been conducted. Although these partnerships focused initially on cleanup issues (two abandoned toxic sites have been environmentally assessed since 1998 and one site has undergone a $1 million voluntary cleanup), current plans represent renewed hopes for revitalization. Proposed revitalization will include housing, technology and job-training centers, and a health clinic. The county has received a $20,000 EPA environmental justice grant, a $100,000 EPA Superfund Redevelopment Initiative grant, and an EPA Brownfields Pilot Grant. The community also has received financial assistance support through the efforts of Senator Ernest Hollings' office. In addition, Representative Jim DeMint has expressed interest in providing support. The Ford Foundation is planning to support to local leadership development and evaluation efforts. Through a collaborative effort, the groups will be able to

WHERE IS THE PARTICIPATING COMMUNITY?

The City of Spartanburg, South Carolina has a population of 43,687. Approximately 53% of the population is white and 46% is African American. The target area, Arkwright/Forest Park on the south side of the city, has a 96% African American population.

INDIVIDUAL INTERAGENCY DEMONSTRATION PROJECT REPORTS

avoid redundancy and maximize the use of private monies and public grant dollars to best help this environmental justice community.

Intended Project Benefits

- Creation of housing, a technology center, a regional health clinic, and a job training center.
- Education of stakeholders in the fundamentals and impacts of brownfields cleanup and redevelopment.
- Development of greater understanding and trust among diverse stakeholders to result in more effective targeting and leveraging of resources.
- Building of local commitment and partnerships for beneficial community redevelopment.
- Education of the partnership on sustainable reuse tools and cleanup funding mechanisms.
- Lay the foundation for re-examining future development and growth.
- Facilitation of job training efforts.
- Continuation of the development of recommendations for a revitalization process through structured dialogues and facilitated charettes.

Project Milestones

- Establish broad based public-private partnership established, chaired by Re-Genesis, City of Spartanburg, and County of Spartanburg.
- Begin cleanup of two Superfund sites and other contaminated industrial properties.
- Create, using planning charettes, a well articulated community vision of redevelopment and revitalization, to include housing, technology & job-training center, greenway development, and health clinic.
- Commitment to providing assistance in addressing transportation, housing, health, and energy concerns from federal agencies, including: Environmental Protection Agency; Department of Transportation; Department of Housing and Urban Development; National Institute for Environmental Health Sciences; Agency for Toxic Substances and Disease Registry; and Department of Energy.
- Plan facilitated conflict resolution with industrial firms.
- Secure commitments of more than $1 million in federal-private funding, including the Ford Foundation.

Lessons Learned

This project demonstrates the importance of dynamic local leaders who have the talent, willingness and perseverance to build collaborative relationships with all parties to engage in constructive problem-solving. Because of this, the local community–in partnership with local city and county officials–has developed a well articulated vision of holistic community revitalization. Providing support for and nurture of such local leaders is a critical component for successful development of collaborative models to address environmental justice issues. Part of that support is providing a framework around which such leaders can operate. For example, the IWG demonstration project provides a vehicle for bringing together needed governmental agencies at all levels, business and industry, non-governmental organizations and other local leaders around the common goal of bettering the environment, economy, and quality of life of the Arkwright/Forest Park communities. The work of Re-Genesis has now been recognized by many, including an EPA Environmental Merit Award.

Appendix II

INDIVIDUAL INTERAGENCY DEMONSTRATION PROJECT REPORTS

Partners

Re-Genesis; City of Spartanburg; County of Spartanburg (Community and Economic Development Division, Transportation Planning); First Federal Bank; First South Bank; South Carolina Department of Health and Environmental Control; South Carolina Economic Development Administration; Spartanburg

Development Council; University of South Carolina; Vigindustries/International Minerals and Chemical Corporation; Wachovia Bank, Senator Ernest Hollings; Representative Jim DeMint Environmental Protection Agency; Department of Transportation; Department of Housing and Urban Development; Department of Energy; National Institute for Environmental Health Sciences; Agency for Toxic Substances and Disease Registry.

INDIVIDUAL INTERAGENCY DEMONSTRATION PROJECT REPORTS

Protecting Community Health and Reducing Toxic Air Exposure through Collaborative Partnerships in Barrio Logan

San Diego, California   *Lead Agency: Environmental Protection Agency*

The project seeks to identify, mobilize and coordinate federal, state, local and community resources to improve air quality, and community and public health–especially children's health–in the Barrio Logan community of San Diego, California. As a result of a facilitated partnership agreement process, twenty community, business, academic and governmental organizations formally agreed to form a partnership. These organizations agreed on three goals: (1) Reduce exposure of residents to air pollution, (2) Reduce incompatible land uses in Barrio Logan and Logan Heights, and (3) Improve children's health by improving the ambient environment, as well as reducing exposure of children to health risks within the home, schools, and the community. The project partners have agreed that their efforts will be action-oriented and focus on solving problems.

The residents of Barrio Logan in San Diego, California are 85% Latino and 40% of households there have incomes below the state's poverty level. The community borders an industrial area on San Diego Bay and is considered to have some of the worst air pollution in San Diego County. Barrio Logan is plagued by substandard housing, overcrowded schools, inadequate health care and social services, and high unemployment. Criss-crossed by two major freeways, this community receives several million pounds of toxic air pollutants each year from numerous waste storage facilities, large shipyards, naval installations, and small industries situated next to homes. The high incidence of diagnosed and probable asthma (20% in Barrio Logan compared to a national average of 7%) and other respiratory illnesses in children here may be related to poor air quality. The respiratory health hazard index projected from the EPA Cumulative Exposure Project for the area is up to 200 times higher than acceptable standards.

The project partners include the Environmental Health Coalition (EHC), US Environmental Protection Agency (EPA), California Air Resources Board (CARB), California Department of Transportation (CalTrans), National Institute for Environmental Health Sciences (NIEHS), US Department of Housing and Urban Development (HUD), Mercado Tenants Association, City of San Diego, County of San Diego, University of Southern California (USC), American Lung Association (ALA), San Diego Unified School District, Inner City Business Association (ICBA), Southwest Marine, Inc., Logan Heights Family Health Center, San Diego Housing Commission, Port of San Diego, and National Steel and Shipbuilding Company (NASSCO).

The project builds upon the many year efforts of local residents and the Environmental Health Coalition to bring attention to and address the above three issues.

WHERE IS THE PARTICIPATING COMMUNITY?

The community of Barrio Logan and the surrounding areas have a population that is 85% Latino. Forty percent of these residents are living below the State's poverty level. The community borders an industrialized portion of the San Diego Bay area and is considered to be one of the most polluted communities in the county.

Appendix II

INDIVIDUAL INTERAGENCY DEMONSTRATION PROJECT REPORTS

Many working collaborations have emerged, such as the partnership between EHC and USC to conduct clinical studies to substantiate anecdotal accounts of the high rate of asthma in Barrio Logan. More recent activities by CARB around air monitoring and children's health provided an important new dimension to these efforts. Air monitoring data is being provided to the community from a CARB air sampling station positioned at a local middle school. CARB plans to duplicate this effort in other low-income, minority communities in California. New organizations to the partnership, such as ICBA, the City of San Diego's Planning and Review Section and HUD represent opportunities in Barrio Logan for pollution prevention, source reduction of hazardous waste, lead testing and abatement, and better land use practices.

Intended Project Benefits

- Building of community capacity and skills to understand environmental impacts on their health and how to effectively deal with local, state, and federal authorities to change their communities and environment.
- Encouragement of local, state, and federal authorities to more aggressively inspect, regulate, and enforce environmental laws in the large shipyards and small businesses that are located right next to residential areas.
- Identification of major pollutant sources in Barrio Logan and help the community/local authorities reduce or eliminate these sources. For instance, Barrio Logan is working with all industries in the area to implement pollution prevention strategies and/or relocation to industrial zones. Also, trucks should be rerouted from going through the Barrio Logan community to prevent diesel, dust and other particulate exposure to residents.
- Showing a reduction in school absenteeism and clinical visits for asthmatic children living in Barrio Logan.
- Identification of a process to allow local communities to have a meaningful voice in selecting their community for the city's redevelopment effort.

Project Milestones

- Facilitation (i.e., the process of using a facilitator) has resulted in formal partnership agreement between 20 organizations.
- Designation of Barrio Logan as model in new Neighborhood Assessment Program by California Air Resources Board (CARB).
- Selection of Barrio Logan as one of six monitoring locations for the Children's Health Protection study areas made by CARB.
- Continuation of the four-year study by the Environmental Health Coalition/USC/Logan Family Clinic partnership to develop community asthma and air quality profile under an NIEHS Environmental Justice Grant.
- Identification of ways to address transportation issues related to poor air quality has been agreed to y Cal Tran.
- Continuation of the "Open Airways and Tools for Schools" asthma education program by American Lung Association.
- Continuation of the mobilization of resources through the project include: NIEHS four-year grant to EHC, USC and Logan Heights Family Health Center ($600,000), CARB Neighborhood Assessment Project ($500,000 to date), EPA Open Airways and Tools for Schools ($100,000), ICBA ($200,000).

INDIVIDUAL INTERAGENCY DEMONSTRATION PROJECT REPORTS

- Completion of a website for the project.
- Application for $1 million grant on lead hazards control for Barrio Logan is made by the City, with assistance from HUD.
- Preparation for a Pollution Prevention Workshop for all Barrio Logan autobody repair shops by CalEPA working with ICBA.
- Consideration of Barrio Logan for the Mayor's new Urban Village program.

Lessons Learned

A well conducted facilitation process can result in enormous benefits. In the case of Barrio Logan, it was capable of creating a "win-win" scenario by combining a community-driven process with the many interests and resources of other parties–both private and public. This is not necessarily easy and requires a highly skilled facilitator who has a keen grasp of the community, the parties involved, and the issues. A formal partnership agreement has been developed, which can serve as a model for other areas. As a result of the facilitation, the organizations agreed to a collective process that includes a range of commitments ranging from sharing data and information, identify existing and additional resources, to resolving conflicts in a positive and constructive way. They made a commitment to think creatively about how to make a difference in the health and well-being of the Barrio Logan community.

Having created a framework that is well informed by community concerns, this partnership is well positioned to more effectively target, complement, mobilize, leverage and utilize organizational capacities and resources that the Barrio Logan community sorely needs. Moreover, it has brought to the table new partners and resources of which many had heretofore been unaware. These include the Inner City Business Association and the U.S. Department of Housing and Urban Development. HUD recently announced that it was working with the City of San Diego, Environmental Health Coalition and MAAC to apply for the Lead Hazard Control Grant program, which could bring up to $1 million to aid in reducing and/or eliminating lead-contaminated dust and soil in private homes in Barrio Logan.

Partners

Environmental Health Coalition (EHC), US Environmental Protection Agency (EPA), California Air Resources Board (CARB), California Department of Transportation (CAlTrans), National Institute for Environmental Health Sciences (NIEHS), US Department of Housing and Urban Development (HUD), Mercado Tenants Association, City of San Diego, County of San Diego, University of Southern California (USC), American Lung Association (ALA), San Diego Unified School District, Inner City Business Association (ICBA), Southwest Marine, Inc., Logan Heights Family Health Center, San Diego Housing Commission, Port of San Diego, National Steel and Shipbuilding Company(NASSCO), Southwest Marine, Inc., and others.

INDIVIDUAL INTERAGENCY DEMONSTRATION PROJECT REPORTS

Metlakatla Indian Community
Unified Interagency Environmental Management Task Force

Annette Island, Alaska   *Lead Agency: Department of Defense*

This project has resulted in the formation of a partnership of federal, tribal and local government agencies and organizations to address areas of contamination and to develop and implement the Metlakatla Indian Community (MIC) Master Plan. The Master Plan will address land use, areas of contamination and future development of the Metlakatla Peninsula. The Annette Islands Indian Reserve is located in southeast Alaska, approximately 20 miles south of Ketchikan. This reserve has been the home of the MIC since 1887, and is the only Indian reserve in Alaska. The U.S. government currently holds this land in trust for the tribe.

Government activities on this land began in 1940 with the lease of 12,783 acres to the Department of War for building a World War II defense base; establishing a minor U.S. Navy base; establishing a major U.S. Coast Guard (USCG) base; creating a U.S. Air Force ballistic missile early warning system complex; and installing a U.S. Army radar/communication system. The Federal Aviation Administration (FAA) assumed 4,880 acres of lease property and ownership of most of the facilities after 1949, and operated Annette Island Airport until the nearby Ketchikan International Airport displaced it in 1973. The USCG continued to use the Annette airport until relocating to Sitka in 1977. The government stored a combined total of more than one million gallons of fuel at several sites on the island. Today, extensive soil contamination exists around some of these fuel storage sites. The existence of numerous open dumps, formerly used by federal agencies, pose an environmental and community health risk. In addition, lead, asbestos, and oils containing polychlorinated biphenyls (PCBs) have been found at building sites formerly leased by the government where abandoned government vehicles, airplane parts, drums, and other wastes now sit. To date, five federal agencies (Department of Defense, Bureau of Indian Affairs, Federal Aviation Administration, Environmental Protection Agency, and U.S. Coast Guard) have been involved in investigation and cleanup of contamination on the Reserve.

WHERE IS THE PARTICIPATING COMMUNITY?

The Annette Islands Indian Reserve is located in southeast Alaska, approximately 20 miles south of Ketchikan. This reserve has been the home of the MIC since 1887 and is the only Indian reserve in Alaska. The U.S. Government currently holds this land in trust for the tribe.

Intended Project Benefits
- Establishment of collaborative relationships between tribal and federal officials.

INDIANIDUAL INTERAGENCY DEMONSTRATION PROJECT REPORTS

- Development and implementation of a Master Plan for cleanup, restoration, and reuse of the Metlakatla Peninsula.
- Mitigation of environmental impacts in support of the Metlakatla Indian Community Master Plan.
- Protection of the customary and traditional use of food resources.
- Building of tribal capacity to manage and conduct environmental programs.
- Availability of federal technical assistance as needed.
- Promotion of economic growth through the tourism and commercial fishing industries.

Project Milestones
- Establishment of collaborative relationships between tribal and federal officials.
- Securing active participation of all federal agencies with cleanup liability in the task force.
- Collaboration of MIC and federal agencies to clearly define the Tribe's vision for their community and find cooperative approaches to conduct cleanup activities among the federal agencies.
- Setting of common operating principles for this collaboration has been established, including emphasis on communications and support of local capacity building in form of local hiring and training where appropriate.
- Commitment of $2.5 million in FY2001 for site assessment work by DoD.
- Coordination and establishment of IPA positions to MIC for the Environmental Justice Demonstration Project and the recently designated Brownfields Showcase Community grant.

Lessons Learned
Participants view the building of a cooperative relationship among federal agencies and the MIC tribal government to be a strength of the project. The tribe will benefit through the ultimate cleanup of their lands, and will take an active part in the cleanup activities, resulting in new jobs in the community. Federal agencies will make greater cleanup progress because they will know better the concerns and priorities of the tribe, and can resolve response issues within the context of an interagency task force. Close coordination is the most essential element for success. This however takes a great deal of time and effort to achieve. Working with a geographically remote Tribe in Alaska requires great diligence and sensitivity to cultural, historical and legal issues. When projects such as this one are put together without a long-term commitment, and the active participation of all parties, coordination suffers. An important milestone is establishment of a set of common operating principles for this collaboration. It becomes harder to mobilize efforts and existing resources needed by the tribe.

Partners
Metlakatla Indian Community, US Department of Defense (Army Corp of Engineers), US Department of Interior (Bureau of Indian Affairs), US Environmental Protection Agency, US Department of Transportation (Federal Aviation Administration, US Coast Guard).

INDIVIDUAL INTERAGENCY DEMONSTRATION PROJECT REPORTS

Protecting Children's Health and Reducing Lead Exposure through Collaborative Partnerships

East St. Louis, Illinois   *Lead Agency: Environmental Protection Agency*

Community groups, local hospitals, federal, state and local agencies in East St. Louis and St. Clair County are collaborating to implement a comprehensive strategy to improve children's health by reducing lead poisoning. The project is addressing both lead based paint hazards and uncontrolled lead releases to surface soil. Removal actions, where necessary, will promote opportunities for redevelopment in neighborhoods and eliminate illegal dumping.

The St. Clair County region of Illinois is an area that is littered with idled smelters, junkyards, and defunct industry. It has numerous abandoned, contaminated lots that serve as play areas for the communities' youth and as illegal dumping havens. This project targets East St. Louis and other communities in St. Clair County, Illinois, including Brooklyn, Alorton, Centerville, and Washington Park. Air pollution has been a major problem due to the fact that St. Louis Metropolitan Area exceeds EPA's limit on the amount of smog in the air. In addition, when children living in East St. Louis were tested for lead poisoning, there were four times as many children with lead poisoning than in the surrounding communities, and the rate of lead poisoning was four times higher than the national average.

Another recurring and severe problem in the region is flooding. The drainage systems currently in place were originally constructed to drain agricultural land, not to convey runoff from stormwater in residential and urbanizing areas. The region has a combined sewer and stormwater system that is deteriorating. Impermeable surfaces (e.g., roads and parking lots) have increased the volume of water running into streams and rivers, and pollution from lead, oil, gasoline, and other products on these surfaces is carried directly into local water bodies. As wetlands and forested areas are paved, flooding continues to become even more severe.

WHERE IS THE PARTICIPATING COMMUNITY?

Sixty-five percent of the population of East St. Louis, Illinois is low-income compare to the State average of 27% and 98.6% is minority, while the State average is 25%. The surrounding communities (Brooklyn, Alorton, Centerville, and Washington Park) have similar demographics.

Sixty-five percent of the population of East St. Louis is low-income compared with a state average of 27 percent, and 98.6 percent of the population is minority compared to a state average of 25 percent. The surrounding communities (Brooklyn, Alorton, Centerville, and Washington Park) have similar demographics.

Intended Project Benefits
•   Improvement of children's health by reducing lead poisoning through comprehensive strategy.

INDIVIDUAL INTERAGENCY DEMONSTRATION PROJECT REPORTS

- Characterization of blood lead levels in infants, pre-school, children in K-8 grades and pregnant mothers.
- Availability of appropriate medical care service referrals for cases of high lead blood content.
- Determination of lead-based paint hazards and need for remediation throughout the county.
- Assessment of uncontrolled lead releases to surface soils in residential and school yards and parks.
- Performance of housing rehabilitation along with landscaping efforts and weatherization.
- Completion of site assessments on abandoned lots and follow-up with removal actions and demolition activities when necessary.
- Assistance in building community capacity to recognize lead hazards and ways to reduce the threats to children's health as well as avenues to better communication and environmental decision-making.
- Promotion of a healthy environment for the environmental justice community by offering a greater avenue for residents to become more involved in environmental issues in their community.
- Carrying out of public meetings, availability sessions, outreach parties; distribution of a quarterly newsletter; and participation in neighborhood and church meetings.

Project Milestones
- Leveraging of more than $4 million in funding support from several federal agencies, including HUD, EPA, USACE, and USDA.
- Screening of over 3,000 children ages 0-12 for blood lead.
- Initiation of sampling and mapping of areas with lead in soil along with lead blood data correlations.
- Production of educational materials such as video, newsletter, Collaborative brochure and children's coloring book.
- Development of a comprehensive communications strategy for outreach and education.
- Expansion of activities to include towns surrounding East St. Louis.
- Training of rehabilitation contractors, trained as lead supervisors.
- Awarding of $200,000 EPA Brownfields Job Training Grant to a local community college.
- Awarding of a Superfund Job Training Initiative to the Sauget Superfund site, located right outside of East St. Louis. Over 20 East St. Louis residents will receive the training.
- Awarding of a $50,000 grant to local non-profit by USDA, to conduct phytoremediation.
- Designation of East St. Louis as Brownfields Showcase Community.
- Awarding of a $250,000 Planning Assistance grant to East St. Louis by USACE, to assist with brownfields efforts. The City matched the amount with another $250,000.
- Awarding of a $50,000 grant by EPA Region 5, to St. Clair County, to address lead contaminated abandoned buildings in Washington Park.
- Awarding of a $15,000 and $25,000 grant, by EPA Region 5, to St. Clair County's Lead Hazard Control for a Comprehensive Lead Outreach and Education Campaign.
- Planning of a study by Southern Illinois University at Edwardsville Institute for Urban Research, to examine the causes and effects of lead poisoning with particular emphasis

INDIVIDUAL INTERAGENCY DEMONSTRATION PROJECT REPORTS

on educational achievement, diagnosis of learning disabilities and other physical and mental illness.
- Garnering of support from State (Illinois EPA), as a vital and proactive partner.

Lessons Learned

An especially well organized project, with a strong partnership emanating from its partners among federal, state and local government, local health care institutions, schools and neighborhood organization, this project has gone beyond lead screening and abatement as its primary activity to developing a partnership with area Brownfields efforts. Lead is a major contaminant in brownfields in East St. Louis area. This demonstrates the natural synergies between the environmental justice and brownfields issues and the natural evolution toward holistic multi-pronged strategies geared towards improvements in quality of life. The project has now evolved into two major working groups, one focused on health and communication concerns and the other focused on lead remediation and brownfields. Strong leadership has been provided by a leadership core to ensure strategic planning, coordination and constant communication among project partners. Thought is now being given to developing new leadership so that the effort can be truly self-sustaining. One barrier to this is the fact that all partners are so busy carrying their respective areas of responsibility and there is no local entity or position that sees itself as performing this vital facilitation and coordination role for all facets of the ongoing and newly developing projects.

Partners

St. Mary's Hospital Corporate Health Center, Neighbors United for Progress, St. Clair County Intergovernmental Grants Department, E. Side Local Health District, East-West Gateway Coordinating Council, East St. Louis Community Development Block Grant Office, Army Corps of Engineers, Department of Housing and Urban Development, U.S. Environmental Protection Agency, Illinois Department of Public Health, Illinois Environmental Protection Agency, US Dept. of Agriculture / Natural Resources Conservation Service, Southwestern Illinois Resource Conservation and Development, Neighborhood Law Office, Neighborhood Technical Assistance Center, St. Clair County Health Dept., St. Louis Community College, Southern Illinois University of Illinois at Edwardsville, and East St. Louis School District 189.

INDIVIDUAL INTERAGENCY DEMONSTRATION PROJECT REPORTS

New Madrid County Tri-Community Child Health Champion Campaign

New Madrid County, Missouri   *Lead Agency: Environmental Protection Agency*

An EPA-USDA partnership works with state and local agencies to address three areas that impact children's health: lead, asthma/allergies, and water quality. The projects came about when three rural towns in New Madrid County, Missouri, saw the potential benefits of working together. A subsequent request to federal and state agencies for assistance resulted in this project. While community education and capacity building is an ongoing part of this project, efforts will include proactive actions such as planting trees to decrease dust contaminants and improving stormwater drainage.

EPA Region 7 and the Natural Resource Conservation Service Midwest Region have fostered partnerships based on their commitment to ensure that all communities receive the benefits of their programs and that no portion of the population be disproportionately impacted in a negative way by their policies, programs, and procedures. The first area in which these two organizations concentrated their efforts was in three small towns located in the bootheel of Missouri. The project began by identifying environmental hazards that might place community members (with an emphasis on children) at a health risk. Data were also collected to evaluate whether there was disproportionate risk in these three communities compared to the rest of the state to consider environmental justice.

The resulting New Madrid County Tri-Community (NMCTC) Child Health Champion Campaign is a community-led initiative with a variety of local and regional partners. Community development, leadership, and capacity-building skills are integral parts of this project and essential to the sustainability of any efforts undertaken. Data collection, communication, and coordination by all of the partners resulted in the completion of an Action Plan in 1999. Implementation of this plan is expected to take place beginning in 2000 and continuing through 2001.

The City of Lilbourn, City of Howardville, and Village of North Lilbourn are rural agricultural communities located in the bootheel region of Missouri, approximately 175 miles south of St. Louis. These towns do not have the types of businesses or industry established that might make them sustainable, and they are characterized by gross poverty and substandard housing conditions. This project will benefit the community by providing a safer environment for children, greater community awareness regarding health hazard prevention, and a greater capacity to address needs and concerns on a local level.

WHERE IS THE PARTICIPATING COMMUNITY?

The City of Lilbourn, City of Howardville, and Village of North Lilbourn are rural agricultural communities located in the "bootheal" region of Missouri. They are about 175 miles south of St. Louis. These towns do not have the types of businesses or industry established that might make them sustainable and they are characterized by gross poverty and substandard housing conditions. This project will benefit the communities by providing a safer environment for children, greater community awareness regarding health hazard prevention, and a greater capacity to address needs and concerns on a local level.

INDIVIDUAL INTERAGENCY DEMONSTRATION PROJECT REPORTS

Intended Project Benefits
- Screening/testing of children in the target communities for lead poisoning;
- Providing appropriate medical care service referrals for cases of high lead blood content;
- Providing education and awareness regarding the environmental health hazards of chemical products, tobacco smoke, home insect allergens, and field and agricultural dust;
- Planting evergreens, and long-lived trees and shrubs in areas around schools and children's playgrounds to decrease dust contaminants;
- Providing educational materials and training workshops concerning safe drinking water, stagnant water, water sampling and also the signs/symptoms of the ill health effects due to contaminated water;
- Building capacity in the community to recognize environmental hazards and ways to reduce those threats in drinking water, stormwater drainage, and stagnant water;
- Improving stormwater drainage in the targeted communities;
- Taking drinking water samples and constructing a template for a drinking water consumer confidence report; and
- Facilitating the participation of community members in technical training provided by the state.

Project Milestones
- Completion of blood lead testing of children in all three townships involved.
- Conduct of education of twelve community peer facilitators
- Conduct of education of approximately 2,000 adults and 800 children.
- Creation of new community focus on asthma, allergies and prevention of lead in children.
- Application of innovative strategies such as planting of trees to cut down on pesticide laden dust.
- Initiation of North Lilbourn Recycling Project to receive donations of recycled products.
- Initiation of energy conservation and home weatherization project involving ten community participants and services of local carpenter as trainer.
- Initiation of farmers' cooperative involving 21 participants and contract with grocery store.
- Initiation of Federal Transit Authority Jobs Access Project involving donation of two vans to transport local citizens to and from work.
- Initiation of Drinking Water Compliance Assistance Project resulting in $250,000 to dig new well to assure safe drinking water.

Lessons Learned
The project came about as the result of members of three communities approached EPA regarding their individual problems. Their learning that combining efforts will yield better results is a major positive development in of itself. The main strengths of this project are the partnerships between the organizations on the interagency agreement (GRAND, EPA, NRCS), the commitment of the local communities, and the locally-lead philosophy which has been applied. The primary partnering organizations exhibited their commitment to working together by overcoming the stresses which occur when an enforcement oriented regulatory agency, a compliance assistance agency, and a local problem-solving organization come together. While many significant individual accomplishments can be listed, the greatest accomplishment has

INDIVIDUAL INTERAGENCY DEMONSTRATION PROJECT REPORTS

been mobilizing a group of community residents to raise questions about their environment, teaching a set of transferrable leadership and organizations skills, and instilling community pride. Having the community involved in identifying priorities, developing a work plan, and carrying this out has led to important long term benefits. For example, the project has grown from a single project to a full blown initiative, which includes a recycling, energy conservation and weatherization, a farmers' cooperative, a job access transportation project, and drinking water compliance activities.

Partners

Bootheel Lead Nurses, Delta Area Economic Development Corporation, US Department of Agriculture/Natural Resource Conservation Service (NRCS), US Environmental Protection Agency Region 7, Great Rivers Alliance of Natural Resource Districts, Headstart, Lincoln University Cooperative Extension, Missouri Department of Conservation, Missouri Department of Natural Resources, Missouri Department of Public Health, New Madrid County Health Department, NMCTC Community Team.

INDIVIDUAL INTERAGENCY DEMONSTRATION PROJECT REPORTS

New York City Alternative Fuel Vehicle Summit

New York, New York   *Lead Agency: Department of Energy*

A partnership of federal agencies, local officials, and community organizations will conduct a series of meetings culminating in an Alternative Fuel Vehicle Summit. The project goal is to accelerate the conversion of vehicular fleets operating in NYC metropolitan area to cleaner fuels by having communities help in targeting where such conversions will result in significant public health gains. This is intended to result in better air quality for heavily congested environmental justice neighborhoods.

As a member of the White House Interagency Task Force on Environmental Justice Issues in New York City, the Department of Energy (DOE) met in Spring of 1999 with the White House Council on Environmental Quality. Through the Office of Energy Efficiency and Renewable Energy, DOE agreed to lead the efforts of the federal government and community representatives in organizing an alternative fuels summit, focusing on accelerating the conversion to cleaner fuels of fleets operating in the New York City metropolitan area. During the Summer of 1999, DOE formed a planning committee of partners to determine the content of the summit on alternative fuels.

The existence of a planning committee on this issue has allowed the city to talk to community groups about current projects on alternative fuels and has given the community groups the opportunity to express their concerns about poor air quality and the need to do more. The planning committee has given the federal participating agencies the ability to help influence the bus purchasing plans of the Metropolitan Transit Authority.

The communities involved with this project are located in heavily congested environmental justice neighborhoods areas of Manhattan, the Bronx, and Brooklyn which have been affected by high concentrations of diesel burning vehicular traffic. The planning committee recommended holding a design charette to gather additional neighborhood and local and state government input on the issue of alternative fuels. Following that meeting, the planning committee put together an action plan for 2000 and 2001 based on input from participants and included the following tasks:

Intended Project Benefits

WHERE IS THE PARTICIPATING COMMUNITY?

The communities involved with this project are located in heavily congested environmental justice neighborhoods of Manhattan, the Bronx, and Brooklyn, New York City. There neighborhoods have been affected by high volumes of diesel burning vehicular traffic.

INDIVIDUAL INTERAGENCY DEMONSTRATION PROJECT REPORTS

- Hosting of neighborhood meetings to encourage local heavy-duty fleets to switch to alternative fuels.
- Sponsorship of a city workshop on alternative fuel school buses.
- Sponsorship of an airport meeting to encourage more fleets to use alternative fuels.
- Assistance with an alternative fuels workshop for local governments.
- Hosting of an alternative fuels summit to showcase successes and build on this work to lead to greater penetration of alternative fuel vehicles in heavy-duty niche markets located in designated environmental justice neighborhoods.
- Identification of heavy-duty transportation fleets and appropriate contacts in order to get their participation in planned meetings.

Project Milestones
- Commitment of $1.93 million by USPS for purchase of 55 vehicles to electric and natural gas vehicles.
- Identification of vehicular fleets by communities for possible fuel conversion projects.
- Involvement of community-based organizations, citywide, in all planning meetings and design charettes.
- Establishment of an outreach effort to NYC to participate in DOE Clean Cities Program.

Lessons Learned
The collaboration of community-based organizations, business organizations, and government agencies has provided vehicular fleets with a more comprehensive and compelling argument for fuel conversion. Whereas past workshops by government agencies have focused solely on available technologies and economic incentives, the approach taken through this collaborative effort also stresses the public health benefits of fuel conversion and how cleaner fuels will make businesses better neighbors to the communities where they do business. In addition, local community based organizations have brought an immense wealth of information about the issues concerns their neighborhoods. This has included knowledge about how local businesses could benefit from pollution reduction efforts.

Partners
New York City Environmental Justice Alliance, The Point, West Harlem Environmental Action, UPROSE, NYC Department of Transportation, NYS Environmental Business Assoc., Congressman Serrano's Office,.New York City Department of Transportation, US Department of Energy, US Environmental Protection Agency, US Department of Interior, General Service Administration, US Department of Transportation (Federal Highway Administration), US Postal Service.

INDIVIDUAL INTERAGENCY DEMONSTRATION PROJECT REPORTS

Addressing Asthma in Puerto Rico-A Multifaceted Partnership for Results

Puerto Rico   *Lead Federal Agencies: Department of Health and Human Services and Environmental Protection Agency*

A partnership of federal agencies, local health departments, community groups, foundations and universities have actively been seeking effective methodologies to comprehensively address the high prevalence of childhood asthma in Puerto Rico. The goal has been to focus attention on this issue in order to maximize asthma prevention as well as comprehensively address children suffering from asthma.

Asthma is the leading chronic disease in childhood and is a major cause of school absence and functional limitation. The apparent high frequency and severity of asthma among Puerto Ricans in the United States and Puerto Rico is of concern.

Because of the prevalence of the disease, the geographic distance of Puerto Rico to many of the resources and language differences from the mainland, it was decided by the community in Puerto Rico and the mainland that special attention needs to be paid to this issue.

In order to do that and to gain input on the issue a two part step was taken. First an asthma summit for Region 2 (covering New Jersey, New York, Puerto Rico and the US Virgin Islands) was organized by the US Health Resources Service Administration (HRSA) in partnership with the US Health Care Financing Administration (HCFA), the US Environmental Protection Agency, Mt. Sinai Medical Center and the Robert Wood Johnson Foundation.

US EPA hosted a special pre-summit meeting that focused on the specific issues covering Puerto Rico. This was accomplished by listening and interacting to the presentations of the Puerto Rican delegation attending the summit in New York. This provided a special focus on the issue as well as an interesting and productive mix of people working on childhood asthma issues who normally did not have an opportunity to interact with one another.

The summit resulted in two actions. One was a specific action plan and the other was a follow up large community meeting in San Juan. In October, 2000, the community meeting in Puerto Rico resulted in approximately 700 people coming together to comment upon the draft action plan that was proposed by the Asthma Coalition of Puerto Rico as well as to network, share ideas and develop new partnerships.

WHERE IS THE PARTICIPATING COMMUNITY?

The main population that this effort is intended to address is children in Puerto Rico. In the United States, Latinos are disproportionately impacted by asthma. Although within the Latino population there are variations in asthma rates depending on an individual's heritage. A study conducted by the Puerto Rico Department of Health (in collaboration with HHS/CDC and HHS/ATSDR) found that asthma was fairly prevalent among children in Puerto Rico.

INDIVIDUAL INTERAGENCY DEMONSTRATION PROJECT REPORTS

Intended Project Benefits
- Development of a comprehensive approach to treating and preventing asthma in Puerto Rico.
- Establishment of mechanisms to improve health care for asthmatic children in Puerto Rico.
- Establishment of outlets for focusing attention on the issue.
- Development of sources for providing additional resources for the island.
- Development of new partnerships.
- Establishment of an improved monitoring system.
- Facilitation of bringing together approximately 700 people in Puerto Rico to discuss the issue.

Project Milestones
- Holding of the First Regional Asthma Summit in New York, with over 400 people attending.
- Holding of a one day pre-summit meeting with the Puerto Rican delegation concerning asthma on the island.
- Holding of a follow up meeting in San Juan where over 700 community people participated.
- Development of a comprehensive asthma action plan by the Asthma Coalition of Puerto Rico.
- Investment of $1.5 million, by Robert Wood Johnson as one of eight national pilots, in one of the poorest neighborhoods in San Juan to invest
- Conduct of an epidemiologic study by The Centers for Disease Control in conjunction with the Puerto Rico Health Department.
- Initiation of environmental assessment monitoring, by EPA, in two low income clinics in Puerto Rico in order to determine which environmental interventions provide the best assistance.
- Tailoring of its Indoor Air Tools for School program, , by EPA, to meet the specific climatic needs of Puerto Rico and will produce this material in Spanish so it is readily accessible.

Lessons Learned
Many different people and groups were ready to constructively contribute to the effort, because the issue was significant and widespread. Effective intervention can take place because there is a wide mix of people and groups including the medical community, parents of asthmatic children, community groups and the schools. Because the community itself developed the action plan, the sense of ownership lies in the community and building upon an agreed to federal strategy helped to focus attention and resources. Two issues to be dealt with are: the difficulty of coordinating large groups with no resources dedicated to the effort; and the change of administration means new partners need to be brought into the coalition and some other partners move on to new positions.

INDIVIDUAL INTERAGENCY DEMONSTRATION PROJECT REPORTS

Partners

US Environmental Protection Agency, US Department of Health and Human Services (Health Resources Service Administration, Health Care Financing Administration, Agency for Toxic Substances and Disease Registry, Centers for Disease Control), Mt. Sinai Medical Center, Robert Wood Johnson Foundation, San Jorge Hospital, Rand Corporation, Puerto Rico Health Department, Puerto Rico Education Department, University of Puerto Rico, Puerto Rico Head Start, Puerto Rican Lung Association and numerous other community groups.

INDIVIDUAL INTERAGENCY DEMONSTRATION PROJECT REPORTS

Bridges to Friendship: Nurturing Environmental Justice in Southeast and Southwest Washington

Washington, DC   *Lead Agency: Department of Defense*

Bridges to Friendship is a diverse partnership of community stakeholders working together to achieve inclusive community revitalization. It was founded on the premise that non-governmental organizations, private enterprise, the District of Columbia and federal government agencies can better their performance by identifying and connecting existing resources and expertise. The partnership's structure acts as a neutral vessel in which those pooled resources and expertise come together, evolve, and focus on common and identifiable goals.

The primary product of Bridges to Friendship is the process of building organizational bridges and fostering their use—identifying and organizing the sharing of resources and serving as a broker, catalyst or implementer to reach common goals. Bridges to Friendship is essentially the implementation of an agreement to work together. The work of delivering services and products remains to a great extent with the various partner programs otherwise created, chartered or mandated to do that work. This is in keeping with, and helps to reinforce, the concept of better using existing resources.

While Bridges to Friendship is an innovative and comprehensive effort of diverse organizations all working toward the common goal of revitalizing the community, there are many goals and benefits particular to each of the partners and levels. The partnership is pursing these goals through four focus areas, 1) Community Outreach, 2) Youth Outreach, 3) Job Training and Career Development, and 4) Business Development and Involvement.

Environmental justice, capacity building, government improvement and community redevelopment are driving forces behind the project since it began in response to community concerns related to the Anacostia River, federal cleanup and redevelopment of contaminated sites, and the resulting redevelopment of the community. Much of the value added by the partnership comes through capacity building, such as linking youth outreach and job training resources to providers at all levels to create employment opportunities for area residents.

The Bridges to Friendship area of concern includes Southeast and Southwest Washington, D.C., where the Washington Navy Yard is located. This area includes communities dominated by public and low-income housing and is predominantly African American.

WHERE IS THE PARTICIPATING COMMUNITY?

The Bridges to Friendship area includes Southeast and Southwest Washington, D.C., where the Washington Navy Yard is located. This area includes communities dominated by public and low-income housing and is predominantly African American.

INDIVIDUAL INTERAGENCY DEMONSTRATION PROJECT REPORTS

Intended Project Benefits
- Increases in the variety, quality, and quantity of job training and career development opportunities for local residents.
- Greater availability of quality educational, employment, and recreational opportunities for youth living in the target area.
- Support for the creation and/or growth of quality businesses operating in Southeast and Southwest Washington, D.C.
- Assurance that the community's vision and needs are incorporated into Bridges to Friendship goals and area planning efforts (e.g., development, housing, etc.).
- Award to DC of a $32 million Youth opportunity Grant funds from DOL, because the partnership represented a functional system to link resources, programs and people in DC.
- In support of the Envirojobs project, DOL brought in, under the Interagency Personnel Act, a person to lead the project and in addition has hired 3 interns and converted two of them to permanent status.

Project Milestones
- Completion of two rounds of environmental job training this year by Alice Hamilton Occupational Health Center. Twenty-two of thirty individuals trained this year are now employed in environmentally related jobs (over 140 have been trained, with over 72% hiring and retention rate, since the inception of Bridges to Friendship).
- Completion of the work force development manual, "Pathways to Your Future," by the Youth Outreach Workgroup. The manual is designed to prepare young people for the workforce. The workgroup will use the manual to deliver seminars and career awareness opportunities to public housing residents and other community groups.
- New job opportunities have resulted from the continued partnership with Navy and Navy contractors (25 hires, and 15 internships), DOL (2 interns), Alice Hamilton Occupational Health Center and National Park Service.
- Launch, by Bridges to Friendship of the "Columbia Rising" series of community dialogues. The first series is providing an open discussion to address issues and to garner commitments for actions related to redevelopment and displacement.
- Establishment of a process, by Naval District Washington Human Resources Office (HROW) working with the DC Department of Employment Services (DOES), to identify, from the DOES database, candidates as a resource pool for 20 job openings in FY 2001.

Lessons Learned
One of the project's fundamental tenets was, and remains, that the opportunities, resources and expertise needed to address community issues already exist, but in a disjointed, stove-piped or competitive environment. The partners committed to a community-wide collaborative effort and we have followed through. Bridges to Friendship developed a neutral vessel to create opportunities for all of the partners to share resources, expertise and access to decision-makers. Partners who have chosen to make use of the vessel validate this approach as a better way to do business. One of the key lessons is that such a choice, the decision to actively participate, lies with the partner and makes the partnership "real" for that partner.

INDIVIDUAL INTERAGENCY DEMONSTRATION PROJECT REPORTS

This approach has, in effect, helped to mend the fabric of the community. The project has helped to change the way this community functions, the way the federal government works, at least in this community, and participants have changed their methods and behaviors as well. We have bridged diverse cultures of organizations, government, business and citizens so that we better understand one another and better understand ourselves in way that we could not have without working at partnership. In addition to the original "external" objectives, the project sought to develop Bridges to Friendship as an entity and learn from that development. We have learned that the key components of our successes are commitment, capacity, and community champions. Key barriers have presented themselves as issues of trust, capacity, organizational cultures, politics and personality.

Partners
Action to Rehabilitate Community Housing (ARCH), Alice Hamilton Occupational Health Center, Covenant House Washington, Ellen Wilson Redevelopment LLC, Friendship House Association, Anacostia Economic Development Corporation (AEDC), Earth Conservation Corps. (ECC), Environmentors, Inc., STRIVE DC, Woman Friday, Women Like Us, Volt Services Group, DC Department of Employment Services (DOES), United States Department of Agriculture, Forest Service (inactive), United States Department of Housing and Urban Development (HUD) United States Department of Labor (DOL) United States Department of the Interior, National Park Service (NPS), United States Environmental Protection Agency (EPA), United States General Services Administration (GSA), United States Navy, Naval District Washington (NDW)

Pledged Partners
Alexandria Seaport Foundation, Building Bridges Across the River, South Washington / West of the River Family Strengthening Collaborative, William C. Smith Construction, Woman Friday, Inc., The Low Impact Development Center Inc., S.T.E.P.U.P. Foundation, Sustainable DC, Sustainable Washington Alliance, D.C. Environmental Health Administration, D.C. Office of Planning, US Department of Transportation, US Department of Energy, US Department of Justice, US National Capitol Planning Commission

Designations
Bridges to Friendship was formalized (July 9, 1998) to orchestrate community, private sector, DC and federal agency activities to leverage the redevelopment of the Washington Navy Yard into comprehensive sustainable revitalization of SE/SW DC; the partnership was designated by the Navy as a vehicle to respond to the concerns of the Restoration Advisory Board (community representatives); Bridges to Friendship was cited as contributor and model in the 1998 DC "Citizens Plan for Prosperity in the 21st Century"; Bridges to Friendship was designated a National Demonstration Project of the Federal Interagency Environmental Justice Workgroup in 2000; and designated as a US Department of Labor Envirojobs pilot project in 2000.

Appendix II

INDIVIDUAL INTERAGENCY DEMONSTRATION PROJECT REPORTS

Bethel New Life Power Park Assessment

Chicago, Illinois   *Lead Agency: Department of Energy*

Federal partners will work to assist Bethel New Life, a faith-based community development corporation located in the West Garfield section of Chicago, Illinois, to fulfill its vision of turning the neighborhood's environmental liabilities into assets. The project will conduct a feasibility study to determine the opportunities for incorporating energy-efficient technologies. Bethel New Life's objective is to use the existing rail system links and convert a devastated abandoned industrial area into a revitalized economic center that provides much needed housing, jobs, commercial, and industrial redevelopment.

Bethel New Life, a faith-based community development corporation in Chicago, Illinois, is seeking to demonstrate the significant benefits that green development and distributed energy resources can provide in addressing the need for economic redevelopment and critical infrastructure issues, such as electricity reliability, air quality, and transportation. By working with the Department of Energy (DOE) and federal, state, local, and private and nonprofit partners, Bethel New Life hopes to develop an area in the West Garfield Park community of Chicago along Lake Street and Lake Pulaski into a "power park."

A feasibility study for the proposed project will examine the incorporation of distributed energy resources (including on-site power generation) and whether development as a power park would address summer air cooling needs without further taxing the city's power grid or generation capacity. The project might also enable better opportunities for using renewable resources while comprehensively addressing the energy needs of the target area.

The target community—the West Garfield Park section of Chicago—is a mostly African-American community (98 percent) with 40 percent of the residents living on incomes below the poverty level. The proposed mixed-use development would provide this community with a convenient location for resources such as a child development center, a medical clinic, a bank, a drug store, and other commercial spaces. The community also anticipates the availability of Welfare to Work training and employment through building and landscaping contractors at the site.

WHERE IS THE PARTICIPATING COMMUNITY?

The target community, the West Garfield section of Chicago, is a mostly African American (98%) community with 40% of the residents living below the poverty level. The proposed mixed-use development would provide this community with a convenient location for resources (e.g., child development center, medical clinic, bank, drug store, and other commercial spaces). The community also anticipates the availability of "welfare to work" training and employment, through building and land-scaping contractors at the site.

INDIVIDUAL INTERAGENCY DEMONSTRATION PROJECT REPORTS

Intended Project Benefits
- Assessment of the energy opportunities that could enable the design and construction of a mixed-used development in the target area.
- Demonstration of energy-efficiency and environmental benefits of PEM fuel cells used in building applications.
- Completion of a feasibility study to look at how the Bethel New Life property could benefit from its development as a "power park" (in the long term, this study could be used to attract government grants and private development money for investment in this site).
- Redevelopment of the area to include a commercial center at a major transit stop that will provide the surrounding community with comfortable access to the local rail line.

Project Milestones
- Utilization of innovative technology and new urbanist design principles in design of transit oriented commercial center.
- Movement of work on a transit oriented commercial center from planning to readiness for construction in Spring 2001.
- Inclusion in the building of 80 child day care center, health center, pharmacy, employment services, and three franchise businesses.
- Integration of community residents in planning for this project.
- Commitments for significant funding and partnerships have been secured with City of Chicago Department of Environment, U.S. Department of Housing and Urban Development/City of Chicago Empowerment Zone, Illinois Department of Commerce and Community Development, and Chicago Transit Authority

Lessons Learned
While this represents an extraordinary opportunity for leveraging resources and technology to create a visionary model development in a distressed community, the full implementation of this vision will probably not take place. For example, the hoped for goal of incorporating cutting edge energy efficient and environmentally friendly fuel cells may not be achieved because of difficulties in securing commitments from federal agencies. To help overcome the persistent and time consuming problems in getting commitments from federal agencies to make these project work, Bethel New Life has suggested that clear lead agency with local presence and staff time allocation (such as an Interagency Personnel Assignment) would be helpful to moving projects along. In addition, attempting to do energy efficient environmentally cutting edge technology development means sometimes needing waivers, specific funding and approvals that take time and stall the development. However, it is important to attempt these efforts to demonstrate the application of new technologies towards healthier, sustainable urban communities.

Partners
Argonne National Laboratory, Bethel New Life, Inc., City of Chicago Department of Environment, Commonwealth Edison, US Department of Energy, Farr Associates, US Department of Housing and Urban Development, Illinois Department of Commerce and Community Affairs, Illinois Energy Office, Institute of Gas Technology, Mantaky Realty Group, Mosaic Energy.

INDIVIDUAL INTERAGENCY DEMONSTRATION PROJECT REPORTS

Camden–City of Children Partnering for a Better Future
Camden, New Jersey   Lead Agency: Department of Housing and Urban Development

Federal partners are working with local educational institutions in the distressed City of Camden, which has a high population of children, to build the capacity of residents, particularly youth, to address environmental justice issues by improving educational, economic development, and health care opportunities.   Activities include (1) Asthma and Lead Poisoning Outreach, (2) Student Air Congress, (3) Rutgers University Masters Degree Program in Environmental Studies, and (4) Youth Corp Training.

The Camden project has been designed to ensure that the health of city's children in safeguarded for throughout all stages of their development. Manufacturing and related land use account for one-third of Camden's nine square miles, and brownfields constitute more than half of all industrial sites in the city. Abandoned industrial sites contain chemicals, transformers, and other contaminants that pose significant threats to human health.   Through partnerships established as a result of this effort, however, school-age children are being targeted for the Asthma and Lead Poisoning Outreach and EMPACT program, high school dropouts have been targeted for Youth Corps Training, and the Partnership for Environmental Technology Education has been directed at college students. Additionally, opportunities exist for graduate students through the Rutgers Camden Campus's environmental sciences master's degree program.

Camden is the fifth poorest city in the United States and has been characterized as the most devastated city in America. One out of every three residents of Camden is living below the poverty line, the unemployment rate is 36 percent, and the city has a predominantly minority population. Almost one-third of the city's population (31,000 of the total 87,500) is children.

WHERE IS THE PARTICIPATING COMMUNITY?

Camden is the fifth poorest city in the United States and has been characterized as the most devastated city in America. In Camden: one out of every three residents is living below the poverty line; the unemployment rate is 36%; the population is mostly made up of minorities; and one-third of the population is children.

Intended Project Benefits
* Identification of areas of high risk for lead exposure and asthma triggers (through GIS mapping).
* Increasing of public awareness of dangers of asthma triggers and sources of lead and build the capacity of the community to reduce asthma triggers and lead sources.
* Development of mechanisms to facilitate the provision of healthy home environments for all community members, especially for children at risk from lead poisoning and asthma.
* Establishment of effective government, private, and community partnerships for environmental assessment and planning.

INDIVIDUAL INTERAGENCY DEMONSTRATION PROJECT REPORTS

- Monitoring of the completion of all site assessments, make preliminary assessment and site investigation reports readily available, and prioritize Camden's brownfields for redevelopment.
- Identification, compilation, and dissemination of information on lead issues for inner city New Jersey schools in partnership with government agencies and universities.
- Facilitation of recommendations for policy that effectively protect children from lead and asthma hazards.
- Establishment of a master's degree program in environmental studies by work with EPA Region 2, EPA Region 3, and Rutgers University in Camden.

Project Milestones
- Initiation of GIS mapping for areas of high lead exposures and asthma triggers.
- Dedication of the Lead Exploratorium (20 foot recreational vehicle equipped to teach preschool and grade school children about lead poisoning) in Summer 2000.
- Sponsorship of 57 Camden students for a summer youth environmental education program and create jobs for youths by offering a 150-hour brownfields assessment and cleanup job training program.
- Securing of $253,551 from EPA Office of Children's Health Protection.
- Improvements in screening and follow-up care for children at risk of exposure to lead and asthma-inducing allergens and train mothers of children with lead poisoning or asthma on abatement and control strategies.
- Initiation of an inventory of brownfields using a geographic information system in order to provide "one-stop shopping" for community groups and developers on site conditions and reuse potential.
- Bring of the National Science Foundation program to Camden schools, where students are doing environmental assessments in community.
- Development of a complaint referral system for housing complaints the by County Health Department .

Lessons Learned
In Camden, evidence of need is so great that there is heightened awareness and willingness to cooperate. As a result, conditions for the project to succeed are there. However, collaboration among the diverse partners have proven successful due to leadership provided by one individual. A great challenge for this project is developing a strategy to transfer this leadership so that the project is sustainable. The specific local agencies involved–specifically, the Office of Economic Opportunities–do have a comprehensive model in place. However, there needs to be strategies which can leverage support from the parent federal agencies so that collaboration can be fostered in an ongoing manner.

Partners
Rutgers University, University of Medicine and Dentistry of New Jersey-School of Osteopathic Medicine, County of Camden Environmental Health Division, Environmental Protection Agency, Department of Health and Human Services (Health Resources and Services Administration-HRSA), Center for Disease Control (CDC), Department of Labor, Housing and Urban Development.

INDIVIDUAL INTERAGENCY DEMONSTRATION PROJECT REPORTS

Easing Troubled Waters: Ensuring Safe Drinking Water Sources in Migrant Farm Worker Communities in Colorado

State of Colorado   *Lead Agency: Environmental Protection Agency*

A new partnership has been created among environmental and community groups, educational institutions, and government agencies to identify the location and assess the safety of drinking water sources for Colorado migrant farm worker camps. The network created by these partnerships will be used to more effectively deliver human health and environmental services in the future.

Although many health problems found in the general population also affect migrant farm workers, in many cases the frequency or intensity of the problem is greater within the migrant population than in the population at large. Migrant farm workers in the United States represent a diverse group of people. About 85 percent are from minority groups—Hispanics (65 percent), African Americans, Jamaicans, Haitians, Laotians, and Thais. While contributions made by migrant farm workers are essential to the U.S. economy, an estimated 61 percent of farm workers live in poverty. Additionally, migrant farm workers are often found to be living with a number of health problems related to their working environments, yet fewer than 20 percent are served by accessible health care centers.

A 1997 report issued by the U.S. Department of Labor(DOL) found that more than 300,000 workers a year are poisoned by pesticides. A variety of contaminants may affect drinking water sources in these areas, including organophosphates and other pesticides from agricultural runoff, chemicals from nearby industrial facilities, and lead and biological contaminants resulting from structural sources such as defective plumbing and sewer lines. In addition to the direct exposure facing workers, children may also be affected. They come into contact with pesticides through residue from their parents' clothing, dust tracked into their homes, contaminated soil in areas where they play, food brought directly from the fields to the table, and contaminated well water.

WHERE IS THE PARTICIPATING COMMUNITY?

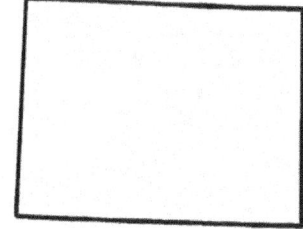

This project will address the drinking water concerns of migrant farm workers in various parts of Colorado.

Intended Project Benefits
- Development of geographic information system (GIS) maps of migrant farm worker camps and water sources.
- Assessment of available water quality data for these camps.
- Conducing of additional water testing for identified sites.
- Recommendations for changes to federal policies regarding testing of migrant worker water sources as a result of data analysis and interagency/worker dialogue.

- Development of an interagency and community plan to address communication and education needs.
- Development of a database to track issues such as migrant farm worker camp locations, water source location and types of contamination, and the number of workers at specific sites to ensure the provision of safe drinking water.
- Building of a sustainable support network to implement policy and communication changes.

Project Milestones
- Development of a database of relevant agency and organization contacts.
- Development of a database of migrant farm worker camp locations and water supply data.
- Development of preliminary GIS maps of migrant worker camps and water sources.
- Sampling of drinking water in selected camps for coliform, lead and pesticides.
- Development of protocols to address unsafe drinking water in migrant camps that receive water from a public water supply.
- Beginning of an educational effort with growers and contractors regarding SDWA requirement.

Lessons Learned
The project has learned that there is much common ground between various federal, state and community agencies and organizations, around which the project can center. Different areas of expertise and knowledge can be combined together to further project goals, and in fact expand upon the original goals. Finding ways of working together has resulted in different benefits, such as the fact that information being developed as a team has applicability to all of the project partners. The project has also discovered that developing a comprehensive statewide database for migrant farmworker camps and drinking water sources is a time-consuming process that must be accomplished over time. For example, additional information that is uncovered needs to be incorporated into the database. The benefits overall have far exceeds the costs. The project is also building sustainable networks to implement changes within this community. We have also realized that agricultural growers have a deep fear of governmental regulation as they have such a low profit margin, that any unexpected cost can put them out of business.

Partners
Plan de Salud del Valle (Salud Family Health Center), U.S. Environmental Protection Agency, U.S. Department of Labor, U.S. Department of Housing and Urban Development, Colorado Department of Labor, Colorado Department of Public Health and Environment, Colorado State University—High Plains Intermountain Center for Agricultural Health and Safety, Cooperative Extension Service, National Center for Farmworker Health.

INDIVIDUAL INTERAGENCY DEMONSTRATION PROJECT REPORTS

Environmental Justice and Public Participation Through Technology: Defeating the Digital Divide and building Community Capacity

Savannah, Georgia & Fort Belknap, Montana　　　　*Lead Agency: Department of Energy*

This partnership of federal, tribal, and local agencies, community organizations, and historically black colleges and universities is working to help communities gain access to information technology and gain capacity to participate in environmental decision making. Federal agencies will provide both computers and technical assistance to establish community technology centers. The project will target two communities: the first in Savannah, Georgia and the second at the Fort Belknap Indian Reservation. These will serve as models for eventual replication by other communities and tribes. Along with federal agencies, Howard University will provide training and ongoing technical support.

In 1992, the EPA chartered the Federal Facilities Environmental Restoration Dialogue Committee (FFERDC) to examine issues surrounding environmental cleanup at federal facilities. The committee made a series of recommendations that were designed to improve environmental cleanup decision making at federal facilities. One such recommendation stated that federal, state, tribal, and local governments need to make special efforts to consult with groups that have been commonly excluded from this process, such as minority, low-income, rural and inner-city residents, and Native American communities. The committee further stated that these groups need assistance to expand and develop their capacities where needed to participate in cleanup decision-making processes.

WHERE IS THE PARTICIPATING COMMUNITY?

The development of community technology centers to provide access to computers and the Internet for these underrepresented groups is one way to empower them in environmental decision-making processes. These technology centers will enable the target communities to participate in information exchanges and policy-formation dialogues. The proposed community technology center three-year project will allow federal and non-federal partners to combine resources to develop model community technology centers in an environmental justice community and a Native American community that will have applicability across similar stakeholder communities.

The project will target two communities: the first in Savannah, Georgia and the second at Fort Belknap Indian Reservation in Montana. A partnership of federal, tribal, and local agencies, community organizations, and historically black colleges and universities will work to help these communities gain access to information technology and gain capacity to participate in environmental decision making. These activities will serve as models for eventual replication by other communities and tribes.

The project will target two communities:　the

INDIVIDUAL INTERAGENCY DEMONSTRATION PROJECT REPORTS

first in Savannah, Georgia, and the second at the Fort Belknap Indian Reservation in Montana. A partnership of federal, tribal, and local agencies, community organizations, and historically black colleges and universities will work to help these communities gain access to information technology and gain capacity to participate in environmental decision making. These activities will serve as models for eventual replication by other communities and tribes.

Intended Project Benefits

- Creation of community technology centers to give communities access to federal agencies and a wide range of environmental information on the Internet.
- Availability of training programs that include computer-based tools: toxic release data; chemical and risk assessment information; and community economics.
- Creation and implementation of youth development programs.
- Availability of economic development tools, entrepreneurship training, and other resources such as proposal writing and grant management to make the technology centers self-sufficient.
- Availability of continuous technical assistance from historically black colleges and universities and other sources via the Internet and e-mail.
- Identification of ways to evaluate experiences and identify ways to replicate project benefits for other communities.

Project Milestones

- Establishment of two partnerships between federal agencies, Howard University and (1)Citizens for Environmental Justice and City of Savannah, and (2) Fort Belknap Indian Community Council.
- Creation of community technology centers by providing excess federal agency computers.
- Making available training programs that focus on computer-based and Internet research, GIS and Landview 3 computer tools, access to information systems.
- Establishment of supervision of community use of training and tools.
- Development of a technical assistance Web site (TechNet) and listserve.
- Conducting of a research meeting with the targeted communities and others to discuss experiences, lessons learned, and implications for the future; and
- Conducting of a research project to evaluate the results and examine the implications for program modification and replication.

Lessons Learned

The project engages federal agencies, tribal and city governments, HBCUs and Tribal colleges, and non-profit organizations that do not commonly work together on projects. By creating these partnerships, the project is able to utilize resources to effectively and economically establish community technology centers. In addition, community excitement is generating other uses for the centers that will help build the overall educational, technical capacity of the communities. One barrier to be overcome is determining the proper process by which to donate surplus computer equipment. For example, every department has different paperwork and requirements and many personnel are unfamiliar with the process, thus creating confusion. The project concept however is broad enough to fit into just about any mission or programmatic goal that an

INDIVIDUAL INTERAGENCY DEMONSTRATION PROJECT REPORTS

agency may have. Through communication and coordination, the project was able to "cut and paste" this project to fit the goals and missions of participating agencies.

Partners

Citizens for Environmental Justice, City of Savannah, Fort Belknap Indian Community Council, Howard University Urban Environment Institute, DOE Office of Intergovernmental and Public Accountability, Environmental Protection Agency.

INDIVIDUAL INTERAGENCY DEMONSTRATION PROJECT REPORTS

Oregon Environmental Justice Initiative

Portland and Rural Communities, Oregon　　　　　*Lead Agency: Department of Justice*

A partnership comprising federal, tribal, state, and local government and community partners will work to accomplish three community-identified needs in the State of Oregon that impact children's health: reduce lead exposure in urban areas, reduce pesticide exposure in rural areas, and eliminate illegal dumping on tribal lands. The initiative will include targeted inspections. It will also include community-based research, outreach, and education projects such as a mobile lab for blood lead testing; development of PC-based geographic information system profile of Oregon consisting of environmental and health databases; community-based environmental monitoring; two federal-tribal-state summits; and "Safe Food"—a farm worker, youth-designed research project to identify pesticide residues.

The Environmental Justice Initiative for the District of Oregon is a multi-year partnership comprising federal, tribal, state, and local government and community partners. Through the support of state government and community-based organizations, the Initiative has generated sustainable support to achieve a goal of the Children's Health Initiative: reducing the risk of lead paint exposure.

By helping communities educate themselves and establish relationships with agencies that can help them positively affect their environmental concerns, the federal partners hope to increase the lead-safe housing stock, increase testing for lead poisoning for at-risk children, and reduce pesticide exposure for farm workers and their children through state-led inspections and appropriate judicial force.

Although the Oregon Environmental Justice Initiative is focusing on the needs of children, farmworkers, and tribes in Portland and surrounding rural communities, the Initiative responds to several important national health-related concerns. This approach to problem-solving, using the tools of enforcement and community-based research and education, can be duplicated and emulated in other Regions.

WHERE IS THE PARTICIPATING COMMUNITY?

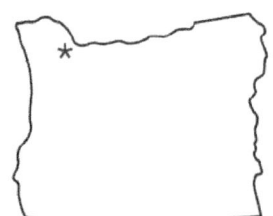

Although the Oregon Environmental Justice Initiative is focusing on the needs of children, farmworkers, and tribes in Portland and surrounding rural communities, it responds to several national health related concerns. This approach to problem-solving, using the tools of enforcement and community-based research and education, can be duplicated and emulated in other regions.

Intended Project Benefits

- Promotion of place-based partnerships with grassroots community groups, local, state, and tribal governments, business, unions, community service non-profit organizations; the academic community; and the media.
- Leveraging of federal resources to address three community-identified needs–reduction

INDIVIDUAL INTERAGENCY DEMONSTRATION PROJECT REPORTS

of lead exposure in urban areas, reduction of pesticide exposure in rural areas, and elimination of illegal dumping on tribal lands.

Project Milestones

- Establishment of a framework for interagency, multimedia, collaborations with communities, with concrete measures of success.
- Creation of an Environmental Justice Working Group.
- Implementation of an enforcement strategy through targeted inspections in environmental justice communities to address lead, pesticides, and illegal dumping on tribal lands.
- Creation of a mobile lab for blood lead testing.
- Development of a PC-based geographic information system profile of Oregon that consists of environmental and health databases.
- Hosting of summits of local, state, and federal representatives with community presenters.
  Institution of community-based environmental monitoring.
- Implementation of the "Safe Food" project, which will assist in identifying pesticide residues in the home; measure levels of exposure to pesticides in food, water, and the immediate home environment; and assess ways to deliver culturally appropriate prevention strategies in order to increase pesticide avoidance behaviors and decrease levels of environmental exposure to pesticides.

Lessons Learned

Networking with community based organizations has resulted in adequate community capacity to engage in a meaningful way with the government. However this must be matched with equal level of funding and support for government staff. Perhaps surprisingly, the project managers' strength lies in the community contacts they have each developed over the past several years' of community capacity building conducted through community-based environmental protection initiatives spearheaded by EPA Region 10 and the Office of US Attorney.

Partners

U.S. Attorney for the District of Oregon, US Environmental Protection Agency Region 10, US Department of Housing and Urban Development, Albina Weed & Seed Project, CREATE, Environmental Justice Action Group (EJAG), Environmental Justice Work Group (EJWG), Governor's Environmental Justice Advisory Board (GEJAB), King Neighborhood Association, Multnomah County Health Department, Oregon Environmental Council, Oregon Legal Services, Oregon OSHA, Oregon State Health Division, Pinerose y Campesinos Unidoes del Noroesta (PCUN), City of Portland Water Bureau, Urban League of Portland.

INDIVIDUAL INTERAGENCY DEMONSTRATION PROJECT REPORTS

Greater Boston Urban Resources Partnership: Connecting Community and Environment

Boston, Massachusetts   *Lead Agency: Environmental Protection Agency*

The Greater Boston Resources Partnership (GB-URP), an ongoing partnership of 39 community-based organizations, universities, and federal, state, and local agencies, acts as a liaison between community-defined needs and available federal resources in order to respond to critical community issues. In this way it seeks to better utilize existing technical and financial resources. Federal agencies participating as members of GB-URP include the US Department of Agriculture and Environmental Protection Agency. These agencies utilize GB-URP to promote community-based planning and implementation of natural resource projects in selected under-served urban communities.

A key initiative of GB-URP focuses on the restoration of Chelsea Creek–the most polluted tributary to the Boston Harbor–by working with local residents to transform the area into a recreational, educational, and economic resource. In this way, it seeks to improve the environment and public health of predominantly minority and low-income populations. Leadership for restoration and revitalization of Chelsea Creek is being provided by three GB-URP community non-profit partners, i.e., Chelsea Human Services Collaborative, Chelsea Greenspace & Recreation Committee, and the Watershed Institute.

The main area of emphasis is Chelsea, Somerville and Boston. In 1999, Greater Boston's multiracial population totaled 574,283, accounting for 41 percent of Chelsea's and 24 percent of East Boston's populations. The unemployment rate in Chelsea is 12.1 percent, and it is 11 percent in East Boston. Nearly 51 percent of the residents of Roxbury live at or below the poverty level.

WHERE IS THE PARTICIPATING COMMUNITY?

The main areas of emphasis will be Chelsea, Somerville, and Boston, Mass. In 1999, Greater Boston's multiracial population totaled 574,283; making up 41% of Chelsea's and 24% of East Boston's populations. The unemployment rates in Chelsea and East Boston are 12.1 % and 11%. Nearly 51 % of the residents of Roxbury live at or below the poverty level.

Intended Project Benefits
- Encouragement of and creation of opportunities for meaningful community involvement, serve community needs, and provide community benefits.
- Establishment of mechanism for matching financial and technical resources with community needs.
- Fostering of cooperation among residents and government officials for the enhancement of the urban environment.
- Servicing of and involvement of low-income communities and minorities that have traditionally had little access to environmental resources in planning and decision making.

INDIVIDUAL INTERAGENCY DEMONSTRATION PROJECT REPORTS

- Development of a plan for long-term sustainability and improvements that addresses community environmental education and improvement needs.
- Partnering with the Chelsea Creek Action Group (CCAG) to work with local residents to build public awareness, promote public access, clean up contaminated land, and transform the Chelsea Creek into a recreational, educational, and economic resource for the communities and region.

Project Milestones
- Awarding of eleven projects to Greater Boston Urban Resources Partnership, with a total funding of $265,000.
- Granting of funding in amount of $38,500, provided by EPA.
- Beginning of work with Worcester Polytechnic Institute and community partners to create first-of-its kind interactive database of GB-URP funded environmental and public health projects in Greater Boston area.
- Hosting of a regional summit on asthma titled "Environmental Justice Children's Initiative," designed to develop a strategy for filling the gaps in current action on asthma and to emphasize prevention of exposure to known triggers in homes, schools, and the outside environments.
- Beginning of work with community partners, federal agencies, state and local agencies, local businesses, academia to conduct community-based comparative risk assessment for Chelsea Creek.

Lessons Learned
The Initiative demonstrates the value of federal agency partnerships to effectively deliver technical and financial assistance and other services to the public, and involves low-income and minority communities that have traditionally had limited access to environmental resources. The Project also demonstrates sustainability in recognition that many environmental issues may not be adequately addressed without the combined resources of federal, state, and local governments and the capacity building at the community level, in order to develop long term solutions from a "bottom up" approach. Improved communication between partners, environmental and public health fairs, and a broad array of educational resources targeted towards educating the community have resulted from these partnerships.

Partners
City of Boston, , US Department of Agriculture (Forest Service, Natural Resources Conservation Service), US Environmental Protection Agency, US Department of Housing and Urban Development, Massachusetts Department of Environmental Management, Massachusetts Department of Fish and Wildlife Enforcement, Tufts University and the Watershed Institute.

INDIVIDUAL INTERAGENCY DEMONSTRATION PROJECT REPORTS

Environmental Justice in Indian Country: A Roundtable to Address Conceptual, Political and Statutory Issues

Albuquerque, New Mexico   *Lead Agency: Department of Energy*

Federal agencies in collaboration with tribes, tribal organizations, and other interested parties conducted a roundtable to thoroughly discuss and identify means to address the broad range of tribal cultural, religious, economic, social, legal and other issues related to environmental justice in Indian country and among Alaska Natives. The Interagency Working Group on Environmental Justice (IWG) made a commitment to ensure Native American and Alaska Native concerns were not overlooked and that tribal environmental justice issues were seriously considered. However, a major barrier towards moving forward was the lack of clarity on how to properly interpret and implement the principles of environmental justice, and adhere to the government to government working relationship and the federal-tribal trust responsibilities.

The "American Indian and Alaska Native Environmental Justice Roundtable" was convened on August 3-4, 200 in Albuquerque, New Mexico at the Southwestern Indian Polytechnic Institute (SIPI) to address these concerns. Over 150 participants identified issues and recommended strategies to assist policy-makers in the development of a forward-thinking, comprehensive environmental policy that recognizes and fosters the unique relationship between environmental protection, human health, environmental justice, and economic development. It provided an opportunity for communications between federal officials, tribal elected officials, tribal community members, environmental protection experts, state and local officials, academia, business/industry, and grassroots organizations. Impetus for this roundtable came as a request during the July 1999 conference, "Environmental Justice: Strengthening the Bridge Between Economic Development and Sustainable Communities."

WHERE IS THE PARTICIPATING COMMUNITY?

The Roundtable assembled a representative group of American Indians, Alaskan natives, environmental protection experts, legal scholars, ethicists, tribal elders, religious leaders, cultural specialists, policy experts, and others from around the nation to identify and address the issues associated with environmental justice in Indian Country.

Intended Project Benefits
- Greater communication, understanding and trust between and among federal agencies and tribal governments, tribal citizens, state governments and other groups.
- Recommendations for addressing five (5) core issues:
  - Federal government's responsibilities for environmental justice in Indian country and among Alaska Natives.
  - Tribal governments's responsibility for addressing environmental justice concerns.
  - States' responsibilities for addressing environmental justice in Indian country.
  - Implications of environmental justice for industrial development in Indian country.
  - Collaboration of tribal, federal, and state governments to address human health and environmental justice.

Project Milestones

- Production of a comprehensive report of the Roundtable with recommendations. (completed January 31, 2001).
- Continued review of the report to identify opportunities for interagency collaboration to enhance environmental justice in Indian country and among Alaska Natives, by the IWG American Indian and Alaska Natives Task Force.

Lessons Learned

Environmental Justice is a prevailing concern in Indian country and among Alaska Natives. As stated in the Executive Summary of the Roundtable report, "American Indian and Alaskan Natives value the environment differently than non-natives...(tribes) use and manage the environment holistically; everything is living and has a spirit. Thus many federal and state environmental laws and regulations...do not address the needs and concerns of (tribes). Land-based resources are the most important assets to tribes spiritually, culturally, and economically." The Roundtable participants defined environmental justice in terms of injustices. Many of these injustices are due to an inadequate understanding of the special legal relationship between the federal government and the federally-recognized tribes. The lack of understanding of tribal sovereignty, federal-trust responsibility, government-to-government relationship, treaty rights, and tribal citizenship continues to hinder the development and implementation of effective federal programs and activities for or of interest to tribes. Progress is being made, although limited, as more and more federal agencies work to develop "tribal policies" and "tribal consultation" strategies, and provide "Working Effectively with Tribal Governments" training for their managers and staffs. Similar steps are being taken by some states as well. Greater attention and support needs to be given to federal tribal programs and tribal environmental programs so environmental injustices can effectively be addressed. Through these efforts, the three forms of sovereign governments (federal, state and tribal) will be in a better position to more effectively provide for environmental protection, public health, and economic development for all communities in our Nation.

Partners

Department of Energy. Department of Health and Human Services (Indian Health Service, Administration for Native Americans), Department of Interior (Bureau of Indian Affairs, Bureau of Reclamation), Department of Justice, Environmental Protection Agency, Department of Defense, Department of Agriculture, Department of Housing and Urban Development, Bonneville Power Administration, Council of Energy Resource Tribes, Medical University of South Carolina, Lockheed